Modern Critical Interpretations

The Revelation of St. John the Divine

Modern Critical Interpretations

These and other titles in preparation

Modern Critical Interpretations

The Revelation of
St. John the Divine

Edited and with an introduction by
Harold Bloom
Sterling Professor of the Humanities
Yale University

Chelsea House Publishers ◇ *1988*
NEW YORK ◇ NEW HAVEN ◇ PHILADELPHIA

© 1988 by Chelsea House Publishers, a division
of Chelsea House Educational Communications, Inc.
  95 Madison Avenue, New York, NY 10016
  345 Whitney Avenue, New Haven, CT 06511
  5068B West Chester Pike, Edgemont, PA 19028

Introduction © 1988 by Harold Bloom

Printed and bound in the United States of America

10 9 8 7 6 5 4 3 2 1

∞ The paper used in this publication meets the minimum
requirements of the American National Standard for Permanence
of Paper for Printed Library Materials, Z39.48–1984.

Library of Congress Cataloging-in-Publication Data
The Revelation of St. John the Divine / edited and with an
    introduction by Harold Bloom.
      p.   cm.—(Modern critical interpretations)
    Bibliography: p.
    Includes index.
    Contents: Apocalypse, theme and Romantic variations /
M. H. Abrams—The Judaeo-Christian apocalypse / John R.
May—Apocalypse / D. H. Lawrence, etc.
    ISBN 0-87754-916-8 (alk. paper): $24.50
    1. Bible. N.T. Revelation—Criticism, interpretation, etc.
I. Bloom, Harold.   II. Series.
BS2825.2.R38 1988
228'.06—dc19   87–15494
                                                    CIP

Contents

Editor's Note

This book gathers together a representative selection of what may be called the best modern *literary* critical interpretations of the Revelation of St. John the Divine, also known as the Apocalypse, the last book of the Christian New Testament and so the end of the Bible as Christians conceive it. The essays are arranged here in a thematic ordering, partly dependent upon whether the Revelation of John is their exclusive subject or whether they also concern Revelation's influence upon other writings and authors. I am grateful to Daniel Klotz for his assistance in editing this volume.

My introduction emphasizes some of the extraordinary disparities between the intrinsic values of Revelation's text and its immense influence in Western cultural tradition. On a grander scale, that is the concern of my distinguished teacher M. H. Abrams, our leading scholar of Romantic literature, whose essay looks first at what Revelation actually says and then considers how it has been read since.

John R. May discusses the range of Judaeo-Christian apocalypses, with particular reference to Revelation and the Book of Daniel. A startling excerpt from the poet-novelist D. H. Lawrence's *Apocalypse* constitutes a soaring, highly personal critique of the Revelation of John.

Austin Farrer, the principal and perhaps definitive modern Christian scholar of Revelation, expounds "the kingdom of darkness" as it is seen in St. John's "rebirth of images" as drawn from Ezekiel, Daniel, and Zechariah. Our leading critical theorist, Northrop Frye, analyzes the crucial place of the Apocalypse of John in the typology of the Bible, that "Great Code of Art," as William Blake called it.

Adela Yarbro Collins centers upon St. John's rhetoric, and upon figures of catharsis or psychic and spiritual purgation in particular. In this book's final essay, Elinor S. Shaffer returns us full circle to M. H. Abrams's initial emphasis, as she too studies the immensely rich Romantic variations upon the Apocalypse of St. John the Divine.

Introduction

The first Christians evidently were apocalyptic Jews who expected the return of Jesus and an end to time within the span of their own lives. "Uncovering" is the meaning of the Greek *apocalypsis,* or, in American, "taking off the lid." The Book of Daniel, composed during the rebellion of the Maccabeans against Hellenistic Syria, is the archetype for all later apocalypses, including the Revelation of St. John the Divine. Christian tradition holds that the emperor Domitian exiled St. John to the island of Patmos in the Aegean in 95 C.E. Two years later, Nerva was emperor and John returned from his rocky exile to the churches of Asia Minor.

Though some scholars have identified John of Patmos with the author of the Fourth Gospel, a close reading of Revelation and the Gospel of John in the original will show such a contention to be highly unlikely. The Gospel of John, unhappy as it may make a Jewish critic like myself, is powerfully composed, but Revelation is poorly written in the original, with its author rather awkwardly trying to get his Aramaic syntax into a Greek vocabulary. No other work in the New Testament benefits so enormously from translation.

The overt genre of Revelation is the Pauline epistle, but the true patterns for John of Patmos are set by the authors of Daniel and Ezekiel and Zechariah, since Revelation is a jigsaw puzzle in which nearly all the pieces are torn away from their contexts in those three books of the Hebrew Bible. This accounts for the odd detachment of Revelation from the rest of the New Testament. The precursor texts for John of Patmos are in Hebrew and Aramaic, not in Greek. Yet the books of Daniel and the prophets do not contextualize Revelation; it is nowhere close to being as coherent or sane as the works that inspired it.

The influence of Revelation is out of all proportion to its literary

1

strength or spiritual value. Not only has it engrossed the quacks and cranks of all ages down to the present moment, but it has haunted the greatest poets, from Dante and Spenser through Milton to Blake and Shelley. The apocalyptic genre in Western literature always returns to Revelation rather than to Daniel and Zechariah. From Melville to Pynchon, American visionaries are shadowed by Revelation, and any student of English poetry or American fiction needs to achieve some sense of the peculiar rhapsody attributed to John of Patmos.

The Epistle to the Hebrews seems to hover in John's consciousness as his interpretive model for how to read the Hebrew Bible, or, rather, not so much the Hebrew Bible or its Aramaic paraphrase as a curious work still called the "Old Testament" by Christians. The Hebrew Bible ends with Second Chronicles and its great injunction to rebuild Jerusalem: "Let us go up," but the Old Testament concludes with the belated prophet Malachi, whose God urges the hearts of children and of their fathers to turn to one another, "lest I come and smite the earth with a curse." The New Testament strives to accomplish that turning by interpretation or typology, in which every crucial passage in the Old Testament is supposedly "fulfilled" by a passage in the New. Typology is frequently regarded by scholars as a benign or even technical matter, but it is the most extreme instance I know of the exercise of the will to power over a text. Nietzsche's question is precisely relevant to every author of the New Testament: "Who is the interpreter and what power does he seek to gain over the text?"

Typology, as discussed by many of our most eminent critics—Erich Auerbach, Northrop Frye, Charles Singleton, John Freccero—takes on a positive aura, but it is polemical in the extreme. Here is Frye introducing it as though it were amiable indeed:

> Everything that happens in the Old Testament is a "type" or adumbration of something that happens in the New Testament, and the whole subject is therefore called typology, though it is typology in a special sense. Paul speaks in Romans 5:14 of Adam as a *typos* of Christ; the Vulgate renders *typos* here as "forma," but the Authorized Version's "figure" reflects the fact that "figura" had come to be the standard Latin equivalent of *typos*. What happens in the New Testament constitutes an "antitype," a realized form, of something foreshadowed in the Old Testament.

The Hebrew Bible thus becomes a giant *typos* or *figura,* a mere foreshadowing that achieves realized form in the New Testament. But no text actually "fulfills" another text, particularly if the earlier text is stronger. Dante is so strong a poet that he persuades us his Virgil is the fulfillment of which the actual Virgil is the *figura,* but John of Patmos is a weak if hysterical poet, and his Daniel, his Ezekiel, and his Zechariah are travesties of the actual prophetic texts. Still, we do not read Revelation, even in the Authorized Version, for spiritual insight unless we are believers. If you believe that Revelation is the literal truth, then the aesthetic or even the spiritual insights are of course not issues at all. But *literary* criticism of the Bible, still in its infancy, needs to ask evaluative questions, *pace* Northrop Frye. Austin Farrer, Revelation's classic exegete, views typology as "a rebirth of images," but such a judgment is an act of faith, not of criticism:

> Since the process is of the rebirth of images, it is to the matrix of images, the Old Testament, that the Spirit continually leads: for here are the images awaiting rebirth; all this is Christ, could we but see how and why; the Spirit will teach us. The work of reinterpretation may include much hard and close intellectual effort, there is nothing dreamy or sentimental about it; but it is obvious that the calculative reason alone can do nothing here. The images must live again in the mind, with the life of the image of Christ: that is inspiration.
>
> The rebirth of images can be studied everywhere in the New Testament, but nowhere can we get so deep into the heart of the process as we can in St John's Apocalypse. For nowhere else have we a writing which is so simply devoted to the liberation of the images as this is. The Evangelists clothe their history with the images, but they are restricted by the historical actuality upon which they fit them. The Epistles find their inspiration in the images, but they express them only in so far as serves the purpose of instruction or exhortation. But the Apocalypse writes of heaven and things to come, that is, of a realm which has no shape at all but that which the images give it. In this room the image may grow to the fulness of its inborn nature, like a tree in a wide meadow.
>
> (*A Rebirth of Images*)

If this were said of Dante's *Paradiso,* it would be said to some purpose. My point is not to quarrel with Farrer's distinguished study, but is to suggest that the issue indeed is aesthetic. Since no text fulfills but rather revises another, the question of Revelation's relation to its precursors becomes the agonistic triple query that always marks the Sublime: more? equal to? less than? Any good reader free of extra-aesthetic beliefs would have no difficulty in measuring Revelation's images against those of its prophetic precursors.

Religious history and its contingencies allow us no choice; St. John's Apocalypse is a permanent part of our literary culture. Lurid and inhumane, its influence has been pernicious, yet inescapable. Frye calls it one of the "nightmares of anxiety and triumph," and one may wonder whether this is either an achieved anxiety or an achieved triumph:

> And there came one of the seven angels which had the seven vials, and talked with me, saying unto me, Come hither; I will shew unto thee the judgment of the great whore that sitteth upon many waters:
>
> With whom the kings of the earth have committed fornication, and the inhabitants of the earth have been made drunk with the wine of her fornication.
>
> So he carried me away in the spirit into the wilderness: and I saw a woman sit upon a scarlet coloured beast, full of names of blasphemy, having seven heads and ten horns.
>
> And the woman was arrayed in purple and scarlet colour, and decked with gold and precious stones and pearls, having a golden cup in her hand full of abominations and filthiness of her fornication:
>
> And upon her forehead *was* a name written, MYSTERY, BABYLON THE GREAT, THE MOTHER OF HARLOTS AND ABOMINATIONS OF THE EARTH.
>
> And I saw the woman drunken with the blood of the saints, and with the blood of the martyrs of Jesus: and when I saw her, I wondered with great admiration.
>
> (Rev. 17:1–6)

I cannot reread this without remembering the judgment upon it of a great Protestant sensibility, D. H. Lawrence: "The Apocalypse does not worship power. It wants to murder the powerful, to seize power itself, the weakling." Nietzsche's pale ascetic priest exalting resentment could not be better exemplified than he is by John of Patmos. Resentment and not love is the teaching of the Revelation of St. John the Divine. It is a book without wisdom, goodness, kindness, or affection of any kind.

Perhaps it is appropriate that a celebration of the end of the world should be not only barbaric but scarcely literate. Where the substance is so inhumane, who would wish the rhetoric to be more persuasive, or the vision to be more vividly realized?

Apocalypse: Theme and Romantic Variations

M. H. Abrams

Near the end of his life D. H. Lawrence wrote an extended interpretation of the Book of Revelation. "From earliest years right into manhood," he said by way of introduction, "like any other nonconformist child I had the Bible poured every day into my helpless consciousness, till there came almost a saturation point." The concluding book of the Bible was the most emphasized and produced the greatest effect:

> By the time I was ten, I am sure I had heard, and read, that book ten times over. . . . Down among the uneducated people, you will still find Revelation rampant. I think it has had, and perhaps still has, more influence, actually, than the Gospels or the great Epistles.
>
> *(Apocalypse)*

In some aspects Lawrence underassesses both the prominence and the influence of Revelation in England. The book has attracted the devoted attention, within as well as outside the Established Church, of some of the greatest English scholars, and of the greatest scientists as well; both Newton, for example, and Joseph Priestley wrote more extensively on the prophecies of Revelation than on the physical sciences. The influence of Revelation also extends far beyond "uneducated people" who believe in the literal truth of its apocalyptic predictions. For whether we are believers or unbelievers, uneducated or learned, we, like our Western ancestors over the last two millennia, continue to live in a pervasively biblical culture, in which theological formulas are implicated in our or-

From *The Correspondent Breeze: Essays on English Romanticism.* © 1984 by M. H. Abrams and Jack Stillinger. Norton, 1984.

dinary language and we tend to mistake our inherited categories for the constitution of the world and the universal forms of thought. A century and a half ago Pierre Proudhon, the radical economic and social theorist, and himself an advocate of "humanitarian atheism," acknowledged the inescapability of religious concepts and patterns of thinking. He was, he said,

> forced to proceed like the materialist—that is, by observation and experience—and to conclude in the language of the believer, because there is no other; not knowing whether my formulas, theological in spite of me, would be taken literally or figuratively. . . . We are full of Divinity, *Jovis omnia plena;* our monuments, our traditions, our laws, our ideas, our languages, and our sciences, all are infected by this indelible superstition, outside of which we can neither speak nor act, and without which we do not even think.
>
> (*System of Economic Contradictions*)

Many of the schemes and ruling concepts of *les sciences humaines,* as well as the plotting and representation of character in much of our literature, have been shaped by the historical design and theological ideas derived from the Bible and from biblical exegesis. Especially prominent in this biblical culture has been the imprint, in narrative plot, characters, and imagery, of the Revelation of Saint John the Divine. In a number of Western philosophers, historians, political and social theorists, and poets, the thinking and imagination have been apocalyptic thinking and imagination; sometimes directly so, at other times by the deliberate enterprise of an author to translate the biblical myth into abstract concepts and a nonsupernatural design, but increasingly during the last 150 years by a transposition of the theological model into secular terms, in a process of which the author himself has remained largely unaware.

I have been asked to give an overall account of apocalypticism in literary and intellectual history, and to dwell especially on the Romantic period (the several decades after the French Revolution), which has a good claim to be called the most apocalyptic cultural era since the century and a half in Hebrew civilization which preceded and followed the birth of Christ.

I. THE SHAPE AND CONTENT OF HISTORY

Revelation (or in the Greek derivative, Apocalypse) is the concluding book of the biblical canon which presents, in the mode of symbolic visions, a series of events, now beginning, which will culminate in the abrupt end of the present, evil world order and in its replacement by a regenerate mankind in a new and perfected condition of life. The wisdom of historical hindsight makes it possible to discriminate features of Revelation which have been especially potent in forming Western conceptions of the human past, present, and future.

Most important is the conception of the nature of history itself. Like preceding books in the Bible, but more thoroughly than any of them, Revelation is recursive in its procedure; that is, it represents the present and future by replicating or alluding to passages in earlier biblical texts, especially in Genesis, Exodus, the Old Testament prophets, and the apocalyptic visions in Daniel. The Book of Revelation thus incorporates and confirms an implicit design of the course and prime cause of earthly affairs which was soon made explicit by Christian exegetes—a paradigm of history which is radically distinctive. As against Greek and Roman primitivism and cyclism (the theory of eternal recurrence), the biblical paradigm attributes to earthly history a single and sharply defined plot, with a beginning (the *fiat* of creation), a catastrophe (the fall of man), a crisis (the Incarnation and Resurrection of Christ), and a coming end (the abrupt Second Advent of Christ as King, followed by the replacement of the old world by "a new heaven and a new earth") which will convert the tragedy of human history into a cosmic comedy. This historical plot, furthermore, has a divine Author, who planned its middle and end before the beginning, created the great stage and agents of history, infallibly controls all its events, and guarantees its ultimate consummation. As the Voice declared to John after his vision of the last things: "I am Alpha and Omega, the beginning and the end, the first and the last" (Rev. 22:13).

This paradigm has survived the biblical myth in which it was incorporated and has deeply informed Western views of the shape of history and the destiny of mankind and the world, whether in simple or sophisticated, in religious or secular, renderings. History, it is said, "has meaning"; by this is signified that it is not a play of blind contingencies but that it has a plot, and that this plot has a controller who orders it toward its outcome. Increasingly since the eighteenth century, however, the function of controller of history and guarantor of its consummation has been shifted from an external and supervisory Providence to forces which, though immanent within history itself, are no less infallible: an inherent teleology, or dialectical necessity, or set of causal laws which compel the course of events. But the prototype of the Western concept that history

has an intelligible and end-determined order, whether fideistic or natu-
ralistic, is the scheme of the course of earthly affairs from genesis to
apocalypse which is underwritten by a sacred text.

Within this overall scheme the Book of Revelation envisions the
agents and events of the latter and last days in ways which have strongly
imprinted Western intellection and imagination; although because of the
equivocal composition of Revelation itself, and the flexibility of the interpretive schemes that have been applied to its elucidation, this influence
has manifested itself in diverse, and even contrary, forms.

The Earthly and Transcendental Kingdom

In Old Testament prophecy and apocalypses, the ultimate peaceable
Kingdom under divine dominion is to be a perfected condition of mankind on this earth which will endure forever. So in the dream of Daniel
"one like the Son of man," though descended from heaven, is given
dominion over the earth that "is an everlasting dominion, which shall
not pass away" (Dan. 7:13–14). In Revelation, however, the binding of
the dragon and the restoration of earthly felicity under the dominion of
Christ and his resurrected saints will last only a millennium, one thousand years. The dragon will then be loosed again, to be defeated in a
final battle at Armageddon, after which will occur a general resurrection
and the last judgment. The earthly stage of the cosmic drama, its function
in the divine plot completed, will then be replaced by "a new heaven and
a new earth," while a "new Jerusalem" will come down "from God out
of heaven" to be married to the Lamb in an eternal union.

Believers who are fundamentalists continue to interpret this promise
of the felicity of the redeemed as applying only to a supramundane existence in a heavenly Jerusalem, after our bodily life and this temporal
world shall have been abolished. Since the Reformation, however, there
has been an increasing tendency to assimilate the prophecy of eternal
felicity to the enduring state of this world, after it shall have been purged
and renovated. John Milton, for one, dismissed the problem of the location of the ultimate human blessedness as insoluble, and of no great
consequence. Whether by

> its final conflagration . . . is meant the destruction of the sub-
> stance of the world itself, or only a change in the nature of its
> constituent parts, is uncertain, and of no importance to deter-
> mine. . . . Our glorification will be accompanied by the ren-

ovation of heaven and earth, and of all things therein adapted
to our service and delight, to be possessed by us in perpetuity.
(*The Christian Doctrine*)

In the secularized renderings of apocalyptic prophecy during the last two
centuries, the felicitous outcome of history is of course held to take place
on the stage of the existing earth, with the timelessness of eternity translated into perpetuity—or at least indefinite duration—in this-worldly
time.

Polarity

Apocalyptic narrative and prophecy is a chiaroscuro history, in
which the agencies are the opponent forces of light and of darkness and
there is no middle ground between the totally good and the absolutely
evil. On the negative side are ranged Satan, the Beast, and the Great
Whore, "Babylon the Great, the Mother of Harlots and Abominations
of the Earth," together with the earthly agents of iniquity ("the kings of
the earth" and their armies), to whom exegetes soon applied the collective
term "Antichrist." Opposed to them are God, Christ, the "new Jerusalem . . . prepared as a bride adorned for her husband," and the com-
pany of earthly saints. The consummation of history will occur, not by
mediation between these polar opposites, but only after the extirpation
of the forces of evil by the forces of good.

This aspect of the Book of Revelation has fostered a dubious heritage
of reductive historical thinking in terms of absolute antitheses without
the possibility of nuance, distinction, or mediation. Complex social, political, and moral issues are reduced to the two available categories of
good and bad, right and wrong, the righteous and the wicked. Those
who are not totally for are totally against; if you are not part of the
solution you are part of the problem; and the problem can only be resolved
by liquidating the opposition. In the popular mind—especially in countries such as America where there is a long and deep millenarian tradition—Revelation has also fostered a conspiracy-view of history in which
all reverses or disasters are attributed to the machinations of Satan or
Antichrist, or else of human agencies, whether individuals or classes or
races, who are demoniac or (in the secular rendering) are motivated by
the negative forces in the historical process. In times of extreme stress
such thinking has helped engender a collective paranoia, religious or racial
or national, which has manifested itself in crusades, sacred wars, po-

groms, witch-hunts and other attempts to achieve, by annihilating the massed forces of evil, a final solution.

On a sophisticated and abstract level, which is not morally pernicious, the apocalyptic paradigm has also contributed toward a mode of thinking in which all process, whether historical, logical, or empirical, is attributed to the dynamic generated by polar opposites. The translation of apocalyptic dualism into a polar logic of process is especially patent in William Blake, who told H. C. Robinson, without inordinate exaggeration, that "all he knew was in the Bible." Blake had no patience for middling positions, for temporizing, and for what he called "Negations," which are "Exceptions & Objections & Unbeliefs" that, lacking a true opposite, are inert. What he sought was a consolidation of opponent forces into genuine "Contraries," for "without Contraries is no progression"; and "from these contraries spring what the religious call Good and Evil." It is the energy generated by the tension between contraries which impels all development, organization, and creativity. The biblical opposition of absolute contraries, with its destined outcome, was also one among diverse sources of the dialectic of post-Kantian German philosophy, as adumbrated by Fichte, developed by Schelling, and given its final form by Hegel. The driving force of all process—including generic and individual history, logic, and the self-generative, automotive, self-sufficient system of philosophy itself—is the compulsion within any element to pose, or else to pass over into, its opposite, or contrary, or antithesis, which in turn generates its own opponent, in a ceaseless movement toward a consummation which is the annulment, or else the stable equilibrium, of all oppositions.

The End in the Beginning

The shape of history implied by Revelation is a circular one which constitutes, as Karl Löwith has put it, "one great detour to reach in the end the beginning" (*Meaning in History*). "And he that sat upon the throne said, Behold, I make all things new." But the new is represented as a renewal, and the *Endzeit* as a recovery of the *Urzeit*. The heaven and earth that God in the beginning had created he ends by re-creating; Adam and Eve, who have fallen, are replaced by the Lamb and his redeemed bride; the paradise which has been lost recurs in an equivalent state which includes the Edenic properties of the "river of water of life" and the "tree of life"; and men and women shall in the end regain their original innocence and its attendant felicity, for "there shall be no more curse," hence "no more death, neither sorrow, nor crying, [nor] any more pain."

In a number of church fathers the biblical pattern of a paradise-to-be-regained was assimilated to the Neoplatonic paradigm of an emanation from, division, and return to the Absolute One, and gave rise to the persistent concept that the temporal process—both in the history of mankind and in the life of each individual—is a circular movement from a unitary felicity, through self-division, sin, exile, and suffering, back to the initial felicity. This circular course was often figured according to the biblical (and Plotinian) metaphor of the *peregrinatio vitae,* and to it was adapted Christ's parable of the prodigal son, who leaves home, journeys "into a far country" where he wastes "his substance with riotous living," and, penitent, returns home to a rejoicing father (Luke 15:11–32).

In a consequential variant of this figure of history as a great-circle route back to the origin, the blessedness at the end is conceived not simply to equal, but to exceed the innocence and happiness at the beginning. To Milton, for example, a Puritan exponent of the strenuous and moral life, the fall of man was a fortunate fall, not only because it gave us Christ, but because the ultimate paradise will have been earned, whereas the initial paradise was merely inherited. Thus when Christ shall receive his faithful into bliss, the earth

> Shall all be Paradise, far happier place
> Than this of *Eden,* and far happier days.
> (*Paradise Lost,* 12.464–65)

A century or so later philosophers and poets translated this myth of man's circuitous course from Eden to a far happier paradise into the distinctive Romantic figure of development—whether in history, the individual life, intellection, or the realm of morality, culture, and art—as a spiral: all process departs from an undifferentiated unity into sequential self-divisions, to close in an organized unity which has a much higher status than the original unity because it incorporates all the intervening divisions and oppositions. As Hugo von Hofmannsthal later epitomized the Romantic concept: "Every development moves in a spiral line, leaves nothing behind, reverts to the same point on a higher turning."

The recurrent plot of Blake's prophetic poems, as he describes it at the opening of *The Four Zoas,* concerns "a Perfect Unity . . . of Eden," figured as a single Universal Man, followed by "His fall into Division & his Resurrection to Unity." This course of events, as Blake describes it elsewhere, is a spiral progress from simple innocence up and back to an "organized innocence"; or in an alternative description, it is mankind's loss of Eden and his struggle to achieve, by "mental fight," the New Jerusalem, which is not simply the garden of the origin but the great city of civilization, intellection, and the arts. No less explicitly Friedrich Schelling adverts to the language of the Book of Revelation as the ground for his spiral view of intellectual and historical process. "I posit God as the first and the last, as Alpha and Omega, but as Alpha he is not what he is as Omega." For at the beginning he is merely "*Deus implicitus*," and only "as Omega is he *Deus explicitus*." Translated into conceptual terms, this theological representation yields Schelling's philosophic method. "Philosophy," he declares, "opens with the Absolute and with the absence of all oppositions," and its "ultimate destination" is "to bring about a higher, truly all-encompassing unity"—the "perfect inclusion of all-in-one" that is "the one truly absolute knowledge, which is also . . . a knowledge of the Absolute." And this process, Schelling adds, "applies just as much to the sciences as to art."

We recognize a similar provenience and pattern in Hegel's dialectic. As he says at the conclusion of his shorter *Logic:* "We have now returned to the notion of the Idea with which we began," but "the return to the beginning is also an advance." And so in the self-compelled movement of spirit in all its manifestations, whether in history, logic, metaphysics, science, or art, the consummation, or "Absolute," having overcome yet preserved all intervening self-alienations, is that "Truth" which includes in an organized form not less than everything. As Hegel puts it—in an explicit parallel of his conceptual scheme to the "life of God and divine cognition"—the True is "not an *original* or *immediate* unity as such," for which "otherness and alienation, and the overcoming of alienation are not serious matters." Instead it is a circuitous progression—

> the process of its own becoming, the circle that presupposes the end as its goal, having its end also as its beginning; and only by being worked out to its end, is it actual.
>
> (*Phenomenology of Spirit*)

II. Two Ways to the Millennium

The plot of biblical history is sharply discontinuous. Each of its crucial events is abrupt, cataclysmic, and inaugurates a drastic change: the creation, the fall, the Incarnation and Resurrection, and the advent of what Rufus Jones has called "the fierce comfort of an apocalyptic relief expedition from the sky" to establish the millennium. Revelation represents all present-day rulers and institutions as radically evil, and promises that these will be annihilated and replaced by the millennial kingdom. After the triumph of Christianity this millennial component posed an obvious threat to the Church and the established social order—a threat the more obvious because the seat of the Western Church was the very Rome which in Revelation had been figured as unholy Babylon, the Great Whore. Repeated attempts were made in the early Christian centuries to delete this threat by eliminating Revelation from the biblical canon. Much more effectively and enduringly, however, Saint Augustine succeeded in saving yet denaturing Revelation by proposing the allegorical interpretation that the millennium signifies the present, but invisible, spiritual kingdom that has in fact been inaugurated at the Resurrection of Christ. Although Augustine's view became authoritative for the Church, belief in a literal millennium remained alive in the Middle Ages, and was widely revived after the Reformation.

As a consequence, Christianity has through the centuries harbored a strong historical prospectivism—the certainty that, though mankind is radically corrupt and inhabits a vale of tears, the best is inevitably about to be, in this life and this world. This millennial expectation has helped engender Western convictions about the future of mankind which have no close parallels in civilizations that developed outside the Judeo-Christian orbit.

Millennialism, Meliorism, and the Idea of Progress

One such conviction is that the human race is gradually progressing toward a much better, or even perfect, condition in the material, intellectual, moral, and social realms. As early as the twelfth century the Cistercian monk Joachim of Floris reinterpreted Revelation in accordance with a Trinitarian conception of history, dividing the course of events into three great eras: the initial age of the Old Testament Father, the present age of the Son, and the coming age of the Holy Spirit when, by the joint agencies of God and men, all the world will achieve a state of perfect spiritual liberty. Joachim thus transformed the single-fall, single-redemption shape of biblical history into a sequence of three upward quantum leaps and levelings-off, ending in an earthly perfection. After Joachim's death some of his followers, especially the Spiritual Franciscans, converted his prophecy of a Third Age into a militant program of radical political, as well as moral and religious, reform which has had a recurrent influence on revolutionary thinking, particularly in Catholic countries.

The modern form of the idea of progress, however, has been mainly a product of Protestant Christianity. Recent researches have shown that this idea was not, as it was once represented by historians, simply an optimistic extrapolation into the future of the conspicuous advances in Europe, during and after the Renaissance, in science, technology, geographical exploration, and the arts. Instead, these advances in the sciences and the practical arts were assimilated into the inherited theological scheme of historical prospectivism, but in a way that drastically altered both the shape and dynamics of the scheme. For beginning with the Renaissance, mankind seemed to have developed the human means to achieve the promised state of felicity gradually and peacefully instead of by an abrupt and destructive intervention; and in the course of centuries, progress was increasingly conceived to be attainable by purely human agency, and to be guaranteed by the operation of purely natural causes, without the need for an apocalyptic relief expedition from the sky.

Francis Bacon, for example, was one of the earliest proponents of the idea of historical progress, as a destined consequence of the use of experimental science to increase man's control over the material conditions of his well-being. He presents this view, however, within the express context of the Christian pattern of providential history, and with persistent allusion to apocalyptic prophecy. He thus reads the assertion in Daniel concerning "the last ages," that "many shall run to and fro, and knowledge shall be increased," to signify that geographical exploration, "and the advancement of the sciences, are destined by fate, that is, by Divine Providence, to meet in the same age." In Bacon's interpretation of the first and last things, man's fall, in its moral aspect, was a fall from innocence, but in its cognitive aspect it was a divorce of mind from nature, hence of man's original dominion over the creation. Experimental science, however, promises to restore the "commerce between the mind of man and the nature of things . . . to its perfect and original condition." The end of human progress on earth will thus be a return to the condition of Eden, which Bacon equates with the heavenly Kingdom of the latter days: "The entrance into the kingdom of man, founded on the sciences," is "not much other than the entrance into the kingdom of heaven, whereinto none may enter except as a little child." And he celebrates the anticipated consummation in the great apocalyptic figure of a marriage, although not between Christ and the renovated Jerusalem, but between

the mind and the universe, the divine goodness assisting, out

of which marriage let us hope (and be this the prayer of the
bridal song) there may spring . . . a line and race of inventions
that may in some degree subdue and overcome the necessities
and miseries of humanity.

Even in the heyday of the idea of progress in the nineteenth century,
when the sanction of its inevitability was asserted to be the inherent laws
of social development, many proponents of social reforms to expedite a
perfected society continued to use the language of biblical prophecy. In
some part, of course, the biblical allusions were merely metaphors for
secular convictions, designed to make new concepts and programs intelligible and acceptable to a traditionalist public and to endow new ideas
with the potency of an existing religious faith. The biblical language,
however, manifests an unbroken continuity with the origin of the concept
of inevitable progress in millennial prophecy. As Coleridge said of classical myth, which he called the "fair humanities of old religion,"

> They live no longer in the faith of reason!
> But still the heart doth need a language, still
> Doth the old instinct bring back the old names.

The socialist and industrial reformer Robert Owen, for example,
even though he repudiated all religious creeds, repeatedly expressed his
conviction about the peaceful evolution to a "New Moral World" in terms
of the new heaven and new earth prophesied in Isaiah and Revelation.
On his trip to America in 1824–25 Owen declared, in an address about
his social schemes to the President and Congress, that "the time is now
come, when the principle of good is about to . . . reign triumphant over
the principle of evil. . . . Old things shall pass away and all shall become
new." Later he declared to the population of the Owenite community
New Harmony, Indiana:

> The day of your deliverance is come, and let us join heart and
> hand in extending that deliverance . . . until it shall pass to all
> people, even unto the uttermost parts of the earth. Then will
> be the full time of that universal sabbath, or reign of happi-
> ness, which is about to commence here, and which I trust you
> who are ready to put on the wedding garment will long live
> to enjoy.

Followers of Owen hailed him as the Messiah who, in the fullness of
time, had now appeared; and just before his death Owen himself soberly

declared that, in "a calm retrospect of my life . . . there appears to me to have been a succession of extraordinary or out-of-the-usual-way events . . . to compel me to proceed onward to complete a mission, of which I have been an impelled agent."

Millenarianism and Revolution

Another historical concept which, in its original development, was unique to Western culture, is both more primitive than the idea of gradual progress (in that it is much closer to the apocalyptic prototype) and more sophisticated (in that it has in the last century and a half been sanctioned by a complex structure of economic and social theory). This is the concept that both the institutional and moral evils of the present world will, by an inner necessity, be abolished once for all by a sudden, violent, and all-inclusive political and social revolution.

The millenarian feature of Revelation, Ernest Tuveson has remarked, provides a scenario for revolution. And recurrently in Protestant Europe the Book of Revelation, together with the apocalypse in Daniel, has inspired revolutionary uprisings against the institutional powers of evil. In the sixteenth century the Anabaptists in northern Europe, under such leaders as Thomas Müntzer and John of Leyden, "The Messiah of the Last Days," initiated violent movements against the established powers in order to prepare the way for the divine Kingdom. In the English civil wars of the next century, radical sects such as the Fifth Monarchy Men and the Diggers were possessed by the fervent belief that the conflict was the inauguration of the Second Coming and millennium—a belief that for an interval was shared by Oliver Cromwell and John Milton. In the latter eighteenth century the American Revolution evoked millenarian excitement among some adherents, while the early period of the French Revolution was widely interpreted as the glorious prelude to the universal felicity prophesied in Apocalypse—in Catholic France only by a few fringe groups, but in Protestant England and Germany by many of the major intellectuals of the 1790s.

The event of the French Revolution and its European afterwaves precipitated the development, in the course of the nineteenth century, of the theory of absolute revolution, which is best known in the version of Marx and Engels. In its distinctive features, an absolute revolution is conceived to be: (1) inevitable, because compelled by iron laws, or by a dialectical teleology, operative within the historical process itself; (2) abrupt and relatively imminent; (3) effected through the radical and irreconcilable opposition between institutions, races, or economic classes, in which one side (fated to prevail) embodies the historical right and good and its opponent (fated to be defeated and annihilated) embodies historical wrong and evil; (4) led by a militant élite, who recognize, cooperate with, and so expedite the irresistible process of history; (5) violent, because destined to be achieved by a fierce but purifying destruction of the forces of historical evil; (6) absolute, in that instead of gradual improvement or reform, there will be a rapid transformation of the very foundations of society and its institutions so as to effect a state of peace, community, justice, and the optimal conditions for human well-being; (7) universal—though it is to be initiated at a critical time and place, the revolution will, by irresistible contagion, spread to encompass all the inhabited world; and (8) ultimate and irrevocable, in that the transformation of society will also transform those attributes of human nature which have brought us to our present plight, restore man to his original humanity, and thus ensure the perpetuation of the new era.

The certainty that the future will culminate in such a radical transformation, it is usually claimed, is based on valid induction from the historical past. But in its salient features we recognize in the theory of absolute revolution the stark outline of the apocalyptic prophecy, guaranteed by omnipotence, that history, after an imminent and violent victory of a messianic leader and his forces of good over the consolidated forces of evil, will eventuate in an abrupt and total alteration of the conditions of mankind into a state which is figured as a redeemed city that will recuperate the felicity of the aboriginal garden.

III. THE APOCALYPSE WITHIN

The Apocalypse, as Milton remarked, rises "to a Prophetick pitch in types, and Allegories." The symbolic and typological mode in which it is set forth has made Revelation a very flexible text for historical application. The antitype of the Beast, or of Antichrist, in accordance with the time, place, and persuasion of the interpreter, has been variously identified as the Jews, the Ottomans, the Pope, France, Charles I, Cromwell, priestcraft, the alliance against revolutionary France, the landholding aristocracy, capitalists, the American slaveholder, and Hitler; even in a single interpreter, the antitype has sometimes shifted drastically, in consonance with a shift in the interpreter's outlook and preoccupations. This flexibility has also served to make predictions based on Revelation invulnerable to disconfirmation. In the demotic type of prediction—in which the group, having computed the precise date, dispose of their worldly goods, don white robes, and ascend a hill to await the relief expedition from the sky—the failure of the event to happen on schedule usually results, not in a rejection of the prediction, but in a recalculation of the prophetic arithmetic. In the derivative, secular mode of prediction, the failure of a political revolution to effect the predicted transformation in the nature and well-being of mankind leads to the postponement of the change to a secular second advent after an ever-extending period of the dictatorship of the proletariat, or to its reformulation as the emergent product of an indefinitely continuing revolution. In both instances, religious and secular, the capacity of the predictive scheme to survive all counterevidence rests on faith in an infallible but equivocal charter which allows broad play to the force of human desire.

The freedom of interpretive maneuver was greatly increased by the early application to Revelation of an allegorical mode of reading, either as an overlay or as a total displacement of its "literal"—that is, historical—reference, and especially by the interpretation of its "carnal sense" as encoding an inner "spiritual sense." The tendency to internalize apocalypse by a spiritual reading began in the Gospels themselves: "For, behold, the kingdom of God is within you" (Luke 17:21). Saint Paul, the first exemplar of the distinctively Christian experience of conversion, enlarged the analogy to include an equivalent, in the spirit of the individual convert, of a second creation, of a new heaven and new earth, and of the marriage between the Lamb and the New Jerusalem: "Therefore if any man be in Christ, he is a new creature: old things are passed away; behold, all things are become new" (2 Cor. 5:17); "Wherefore, my brethren, ye also are become dead to the law . . . that ye should be married to another . . . who is raised from the dead" (Rom. 7:4). In his *Confessions* Augustine, who rejected the literal reading of the millennial promise, effected instead the full transfer of apocalyptic prophecy from the outer world to the theater of the individual spirit, where one experiences the pre-enactment, in this life, of the historical events of the latter days. Building, as he himself indicates, on the established pattern of Christian conversion from Paul to Athanasius's recent *Life of St. Anthony,* Augustine describes in detail the sustained and anguished conflict between his "two wills" (the inner equivalent of the forces of Christ and Antichrist), culminating in a spiritual Armageddon in the garden at Milan, the final triumph of the good will, and the abrupt interposition of grace to effect the annihilation of the old creature and the birth of the new: "dying unto death and living unto life" (*Confessions,* 8.11).

By completing the process of psychohistorical parallelism, Augustine established the distinctive Christian paradigm of the interior life as one of polar self-division, internecine self-conflict, crisis, abrupt rebirth, and the consequent renovation of the way we experience the world; at the same time, by his detailed narration of these events in the course of his own life, he established the enduring literary genre of the spiritual autobiography. We recognize the mode, for example, on the moral level of its multiple significations, in Dante's account of his toilsome spiritual journey through hell and purgatory to the vision of paradise—a personal, inner experience which is proleptic of what will happen, historically, to all those who shall be redeemed *all'ultima giustizzia* to dwell in that "true kingdom" which is "our city," where at the appointed time Dante too shall attend the wedding feast as a member of the Spouse (*Paradiso*, 30). In *The Faerie Queene* Spenser converted the chivalric quest-romance of the Middle Ages into his "continued Allegory, or darke conceit," of which the chief prototype was the Book of Revelation. In its reference to the historical future, the narrative signifies the events preparatory to the Second Advent of Christ, his ultimate victory over the dragon, and the apocalyptic marriage which will inaugurate the restoration of Eden; at the same time, spiritually it signifies the quest for redemption, the fights against the agents and deceptions of evil, the triumph, and the spiritual marriage which is enacted in this present life within the soul of each wayfaring Christian, including Spenser himself. Augustine's *Confessions* has also engendered numerous spiritual autobiographies in prose; most of these writings are Protestant, and many represent a working-class pilgrim who makes his laborious interior way past the pitfalls of Satan toward the celestial city and the apocalyptic marriage of the Lamb. John Bunyan, who wrote a proletarian form of the Augustinian autobiography, *Grace Abounding,* also wrote in *Pilgrim's Progress* the immortal allegory of the proletarian spiritual journey—a pedestrian equivalent to the quest for an inner apocalypse by Spenser's courtly knight on horseback.

In the central tradition of Christian, and especially of Protestant, exegesis, the spiritual sense is justified as an overreading of the basic sense of Scripture, which is literal and historical. Some radical inner-light Protestants, however, proposed a mode of interpretation which regarded the spiritual meaning not as supplementing, but as totally displacing the literal sense. Gerrard Winstanley, leader of the sect of Diggers—that is, Christian communists—during the Puritan Revolution in England, proclaimed that any reading of the Bible which substitutes "bare letters, words and histories for spirit" is the work of the "great Dragon," for "all that which you can call the history . . . is all to be seen and felt within you." Not only the places, events, and doctrines, but all the human and supernatural protagonists in the Bible, including Jehovah and Jesus, are nothing more than figurative vehicles for the powers and processes of individual minds in mundane experience. Anyone who worships an external God "in the heavens" in fact worships the Devil; also, not "Jesus Christ at a distance from thee . . . but a Christ within is thy Saviour. . . . *And besides him there is no Saviour.*" By the same token the events of the last days in Revelation signify solely a personal and internal experience: "Now the second *Adam* Christ, hath taken the Kingdom my body, and rules in it; *He makes it a new heaven, and a new earth, wherein dwells Righteousness*"; "And this is to be made a new creature." The new heaven and new earth, it thus turns out, instead of being a transcendent habitat that "shal not be known and seen, til the body is laid in the dust," is simply our present world, perceived in a new way by our redeemed and glorified senses:

> I tel you, this great mystery is begun to appear, and it must
> be seen by the material eyes of the flesh: And those five senses
> that is in man, shall partake of his glory.
>
> (*The New Law of Righteousness*)

A century and a half later Blake told H. C. Robinson that "all he knew was in the Bible," but added the crucial proviso that "he understands by the Bible the spiritual sense." Blake's "spiritual sense" is very like Winstanley's, in that it invalidates the literal sense as a fiction propagated by "Priesthood" and internalizes both the divine and human agents and events of the biblical narrative. "All deities reside in the human breast"; all powers to effect drastic change in the perceived world are mental powers; and heaven, hell, and paradise are states of mind:

> I know of no other . . . Gospel than the liberty both of body
> & mind to exercise the Divine Arts of Imagination. . . . What
> is the Joy of Heaven but Improvement in the things of the
> Spirit? What are the Pains of Hell but Ignorance, Bodily Lust,
> Idleness & devastation of the things of the Spirit? . . . to La-
> bour in Knowledge is to Build up Jerusalem.

Blake identifies Christ the Redeemer with the human imagination, and therefore conceives the apocalyptic new earth to be this world, when it is perceived imaginatively—that is, through our redeemed and liberated senses. "The ancient tradition that the world will be consumed in fire is true," but in the spiritual sense that "this will come to pass by an improvement of sensual enjoyment"; for "if the doors of perception were cleansed every thing would appear to man as it is, infinite." It is in this radical sense that "the Eye altering, alters all."

Blake probably derived his version of biblical hermeneutics from left-wing dissenting sects in late-eighteenth-century England. To spiritualize biblical history and prophecy, however, was a common poetic procedure among Blake's young contemporaries. Wordsworth, for example, proclaimed that the theme of his poetic autobiography concerned divine powers and actions, internalized as processes of his own mind:

> Of genius, power,
> Creation, and divinity itself,
> I have been speaking, for my theme has been
> What passed within me.
> . . . .
> This is in truth heroic argument,
> And genuine prowess.
> (*The Prelude*, 1805 text, 3.171–83)

And in the verse "Prospectus" to his overall poetic enterprise, which resonates with echoes of Revelation, Wordsworth announced that his poetic journey must ascend beyond "the heaven of heavens" past "Jehovah, with his thunder, and the choir / Of shouting Angels," and must also sink deeper than the lowest hell; all this, however, without leaving the confines of

> the mind of Man,
> My haunt, and the main region of my Song.

The conclusion of his "high argument" is the recovery of a lost paradise, but a paradise which is the very world of all of us, to be achieved by a consummation figured as an apocalyptic marriage between the prime Romantic opposites of subject and object, spirit and its alienated other—or in the English terms, between mind and nature: "Paradise, and groves / Elysian, Fortunate Fields,"

> why should they be
> A history only of departed things,
> Or a mere fiction of what never was?
> For the discerning intellect of Man
> When wedded to this goodly universe

> In love and holy passion, shall find these
> A simple produce of the common day.
>
> . . . .
>
> This is our high argument.

IV. American Millennialism

Writers in diverse times and places have claimed that their nation is the typological "New Israel," divinely chosen to play the leading role in initiating the earthly Kingdom. The nation possessed of the most thoroughly and enduringly millennial ideology, however, is America, in a tradition that began even before it was settled by Europeans. Columbus himself suggested that the New World he had discovered was to be the locale of the new earth prophesied in Revelation. This belief was brought to America by the early Franciscan missionaries (heirs to the preachings of Joachim of Floris), and entrenched by the fervent iteration of America's millennial destiny by the Puritan settlers of New England. "For your full assurance," Edward Johnson reminded his fellow New Englanders in 1653, "know this is the place where the Lord will create a new Heaven and a new earth . . . new Churches and a new Commonwealth together" (*Wonder-Working Providence*). A century later Jonathan Edwards viewed the Great Awakening as the initial stage in fulfilling the New World's apocalyptic destiny, interpreted in the spiritual sense: "This new world is probably now discovered . . . that God might in it begin a new world in a spiritual respect, when he creates the *new heavens* and *new earth* (*Thoughts on the Revival of Religion in New England*). In our time the Great Seal of the United States, as reproduced on the one-dollar bill, echoes the persistent expectation in its motto, derived from Virgil's prophecy of a new age of gold: *Novus Ordo Seclorum*.

Belief in the providential role of the New World helped form the concept of the American's identity as a new Adam, freed from the corruptions of the Old World. In its secularized form this view fostered the stress, especially prominent among the Transcendentalists, on the American as one who is uniquely able to reachieve the innocent vision of a child, and so to experience the unspoiled American world as a pristine Eden. The militant application of millennial prophecy emerged in the American Revolution, in the Civil War (which produced the greatest of all hymns on the imminent Second Advent, "Mine eyes have seen the glory of the coming of the Lord"), and again in the First World War. In an alternative form the indurate myth of a millennial America resulted in the imperialist doctrines of the American Mission and of Manifest Destiny. We recognize in William Gilpin's proclamation of 1846 the ancient faith in America as the divine agency and initial theater of the worldwide consummation of history:

> The untransacted destiny of the American people is to subdue the continent . . . to regenerate superannuated nations . . . to carry the career of mankind to its culminating point . . . to absolve the curse that weighs down humanity, and to shed blessings round the world!

This awesome mission, however, entailed corresponding responsibilities and dire penalties for failure, as native prophets have persistently warned in American jeremiads that have preempted the imagery of the *dies irae;* it has also fostered a paranoid tendency to blame historical setbacks on diverse baleful conspirators, determined to frustrate the divine intention. And the investment of inordinate hope in the American promise has effected, in times of disillusion, an equal but opposite reaction of unqualified despair. Herman Melville in 1850 had shared the ardent belief that "we Americans are the peculiar, chosen people—the Israel of our time. . . . God has predestined, mankind expects great things from our race." In this "New World," the "political Messiah . . . has come in *us.*" A quarter-century later Melville voiced the depressive other side of America's manic millennialism. Beyond all the saddest thought of old Europe, he lamented in *Clarel,*

> Might be the New World's sudden brought . . .
> To feel the arrest of hope's advance,
> And squandered last inheritance;
> And cry—"To Terminus build fanes!
> Columbus ended earth's romance:
> No New World to mankind remains!"

V. Romantic Apocalypticism: Political, Cognitive, Imaginative

In its founding and continuing ideology, America is the most millennial of nations, but the period of English and German Romanticism, in its preoccupation with the philosophic, social, or poetic seer who demonstrates the way to a secular redemption, is the most apocalyptic of cultural eras. In England, with its inheritance of Puritan millenarianism during the civil wars, and in Germany, with its even older chiliastic tradition and the emphasis on eschatological renewal in Pietist theology, the outbreak of the French Revolution revived the ancient hope. In both countries a chorus of preachers, poets, and young intellectuals endowed the Revolution with the myth of apocalypse, in the excited expectation that this local event heralded a renovated world for a regenerate mankind. As Robert Southey said, in retrospect from his conservative middle age, few persons who have not lived through the bright initial period of the French Revolution "can conceive or comprehend . . . what a visionary world" it seemed to open: "Old things seemed passing away, and nothing was dreamt of but the regeneration of the human race." "Bliss was it in that dawn to be alive," Wordsworth recalled of those years, in *The Prelude,* with

> France standing on the top of golden hours,
> And human nature seeming born again.
> (6.353–54)

Hegel, Schelling, and Hölderlin, while fellow students at Tübingen Seminary, all shared this perfervid millenarian enthusiasm. Looking back, like Southey and Wordsworth, from the standpoint of his later conservatism, Hegel described the effect of this "world-historical" event of his youth in theological terms similar to theirs:

> It was a glorious dawn. All thinking beings shared in the jubilation of the epoch. . . . An enthusiasm of the spirit thrilled through the world, as though the time were now come of the actual reconciliation of God with the world.

Through the mid-1790s the poets Blake, Wordsworth, Coleridge, and Southey, like Hölderlin in Germany, responded to the great events of the time by writing visionary epics, verse narratives, or Pindaric odes which, with a lavish use of apocalyptic symbols, depicted the dark and violent past and present of mankind, then hailed the outbreak of the French Revolution as the critical event which would usher in a new world combining the features of the biblical paradise and the pagan age of gold. The conclusion of Coleridge's prose Argument for his extended poetic vision, "Religious Musings," written in 1794, tersely summarizes this prophetic reading of current events: "The present State of Society. The French Revolution. Millennium. Universal Redemption. Conclusion."

At the French excesses that began with the Reign of Terror, English and German commentators abandoned hope in the imminence of a literal millennium. But as in earlier ages, the paradigm demonstrated its capacity to survive disconfirmation by the course of events. The scientist and Unitarian preacher Joseph Priestley, despite some wavering, insisted near the end of his life in 1804 that the mistake was merely in computing the Second Coming, and that the "greatest of all events is not less certain for being delayed beyond our expectations." Much more representative, however, was the view of Coleridge, who wrote to Wordsworth in 1799 that there had been a "complete failure of the French Revolution," but exhorted his friend to write a poem designed to banish the despair of those who, in consequence of that failure, "have thrown up all hopes for the amelioration of mankind." As late as the second decade of the nineteenth century Shelley wrote that the French Revolution continued to be "the master theme of the epoch in which we live," and that this theme was a central element in what he, like many English and German contemporaries, called "the spirit of the age" with its great "new birth" in poetry and philosophy. But as Shelley also recognized, this theme was that of a failed revolution, the resulting collapse of millenarian expectation, and the need to salvage hopes for the amelioration of mankind. Writing in 1815 Thomas Noon Talfourd observed—and his opinion has many contemporary parallels—that this crisis, which was intellectual and moral no less than political, interpenetrated and inspired the great new literature of the age. In the early days of the Revolution, "all was hope and joy and rapture; the corruption and iniquity of ages seemed to vanish like a dream; the unclouded heavens seemed once more to ring with the exulting chorus of peace on earth and goodwill to men." But suddenly these "sublime expectations were swept away" by "the terrible changes of this august spectacle." And one effect "of this moral hurricane . . . this rending of the general heart," was "to raise and darken the imagination," hence to help "form that great age of poetry which is flourishing around us" ("An Attempt to Estimate the Poetical Talent of the Present Age").

"The Revolution," Talfourd added, "completed the regeneration of our poetry." This remark applies to Germany as well as England, and to post-Kantian philosophy as well as literature. In both countries, and in both the cognitive and the imaginative realms, the apocalyptic design survived, but was given a spiritual interpretation—a new kind of spiritual interpretation, adapted to the social and intellectual conditions of the times. In what Wordsworth in 1805 called "this melancholy waste of hopes o'erthrown . . . this time / Of dereliction and dismay" (*The Prelude*, 2.447–57), he and other vanguard writers undertook to reconstitute the grounds of hope, in a way that would be not only pertinent to post-

Revolutionary despair but acceptable to post-Enlightenment thinking. For an apocalypse by revelation or an apocalypse by revolution, they substituted an apocalypse of consciousness: the mind of man possesses the power, by an interior revolution, to transform his intellect and imagination, and by so doing to perceive the everyday world as a new earth in which he will be thoroughly at home.

Philosophic Chiliasm and Poetic Chiliasm

Romantic philosophers and poets were steeped in the Bible and in biblical exegesis. Schiller assiduously read theology in his early youth, and Fichte, Schelling, and Hegel, as well as the poet Hölderlin, had all been university students of theology. Wordsworth and Coleridge narrowly escaped becoming preachers; for Novalis, no less than for Blake, the Bible was what Blake called "the great code of art"; and Shelley, although an uncompromising agnostic, studied the Bible constantly and listed it as "last, yet first" among fifteen books adequate to constitute a good library.

The new philosophy, like the new poetry of the Romantic era, achieved innovation by reverting to, but retranslating, the biblical paradism of paradise, the fall, the redemption, and paradise-to-be-regained. Herder, Kant, Schiller, Fichte, Schelling, and Hegel (following the precedent of Lessing's *The Education of the Human Race,* 1780) all undertook, as they expressly asserted, to translate the conceptual truth incorporated in biblical myth into the secular mode that the Germans call *Universalgeschichte.* In this historical genre, the vanguard of human consciousness, represented as a single character called "Mankind," falls from the paradisal unity of a purely instinctual life into the "evil" of having to make moral choices, as well as other kinds of self-division and conflicts which, by their internal energy, compel him along the journey back toward the unity and felicity of his origin. To such a rational transposition of the biblical millennium by himself and other writers, Kant applied the term *der philosophische, Chiliasmus.* "One sees," he also remarked, "that philosophy too can have its chiliasm . . . which is nothing less than visionary." In the 1790s the frustrated promise of the French Revolution became for philosophers (including the elderly Kant) a crucial event in this progressive educational journey of Mankind. In addition it was increasingly stressed that man's fall from instinctual self-unity into dispersion and self-conflict was a *felix culpa,* because the way back is also a way up, from a simplex unity to the complex integrity of a superior Mankind inhabiting a paradise happier far than the distant and undivided original. In parallel with this *Universalgeschichte* was the Romantic *Bildungsgeschichte*, narrating, in the vehicle of a life-journey, the educational growth of a single mind; among its instances are Hölderlin's *Hyperion* (1797–99), Wordsworth's *Prelude* (1805), and Carlyle's *Sartor Resartus* (1833–34). This latter genre, constituting a theodicy of the individual life, was a secular revision of the Christian spiritual autobiography. In the Romantic mode the fragmented consciousness reaches a crisis, or spiritual breakdown, immediately followed by a breakthrough to a higher integrity, from which vantage the individual finally is able to discern the implicit teleology that governs, and justifies, his painful educational journey—that is, the achievement of his mature identity and the recognition of his predestined vocation as public spokesman in his time of troubles.

What is less obvious—though the fact was expressly asserted by the philosophers themselves, and reiteratively implied by the design, imagery, and allusions in their writings—is that the great post-Kantian philosophical systems, no less than the "universal history" these thinkers expounded, were secularized versions of the Christian paradigm of the creation, fall, and apocalyptic consummation of history. What Novalis said of Fichte's philosophy, that it is "perhaps nothing else than applied Christianity," can be even more emphatically claimed for the speculative systems of Fichte's younger contemporaries, Schelling and Hegel. As Hegel repeatedly said, while philosophy "must not allow herself to be overawed by religion," it cannot neglect, but must translate into its own nonsupernatural terms, "the tales and allegories of religion."

In Hegel's *Phenomenology of Spirit* the emergence of "the Revealed Religion," with what he calls its "picture-thinking" in "the form of objectivity," is the penultimate stage of the spirit's process of self-education toward a consummation in philosophical *Wissenschaft*. In his narration of this process Hegel systematically translates the crucial occurrences and concepts of biblical history into the conceptual mode of genuine philosophy, which transcends, while preserving its truth-content, the mythical representations of revealed Christianity. Carlyle's German philosopher, Professor Teufelsdröckh, speaks for his major contemporaries when he asserts that "the Mythus of the Christian Religion looks not in the eighteenth century as it did in the eighth," then sets himself the task "to embody the divine Spirit of that Religion in a new Mythus, in a new vehicle and vesture."

The overall plot and critical events of biblical history, conceptualized, thus reappear as the constitutive paradigm in the systems of Romantic philosophy, however diverse the details in each system. These philosophies, unlike most traditional systems, are not static structures of truth, but are constantly on the move, and their movement is end-oriented. In the beginning is the creation, at the timeless "moment" when the unitary Absolute, or universal Ego, or Spirit sets itself off as object from itself as subject. "Thus," in Hegel's version, "the merely eternal or abstract Spirit becomes an 'other' to itself, or enters into existence. Accordingly"—in the language, that is, of picture-thinking—"it *creates* a world." This primal self-division inaugurates a process of ever-renewing others, or oppositions, or antitheses which impel a movement, through a crisis, toward that last, far-off, divine event toward which both speculative thinking and the universe inevitably move. In the *Phenomenology* the Armageddon, or *crise de conscience,* of the self-alienated spirit manifests itself, historically, in the French Revolution and the Reign of Terror. And the goal-event of the process, which Hegel calls "Absolute Knowledge" or the self-reunited "Spirit that knows itself as Spirit," is presented, in Hegel's persistent use of double entendres, as the cognitive translation both of the human restoration of its original mode of existence and of the new heaven and new earth prophesied in the picture-thinking of Revelation. As Hegel puts it in the concluding page of the *Phenomenology:* "This transformed existence—the former one, but now reborn of the Spirit's knowledge—is the new existence, a new world and a new shape of Spirit."

Hegel's *das neue Dasein* which is *eine neue Welt*—the "goal" and "fulfillment," as he calls it, both of consciousness and history that will justify their agonized evolution—has its equivalent in his fellow philosophers. In Schiller's *Aesthetic Education of Man* (1795), the equivalent is the "aesthetic state"; this state replaces what Schiller describes as the "vain hope" invested in political revolution by "a complete revolution" of consciousness which will yield—although, for the time being, only in the realm of "aesthetic semblance"—a condition of genuine liberty, fraternity, and equality. In Fichte's version of 1806, this ultimate state is the life of "Blessedness" which Fichte substitutes for his earlier millenarian hope in the French Revolution; this "Doctrine of Blessedness," he now asserts, "can be nothing else than a Doctrine of Knowledge," by means of which we will achieve "the new world which rises before us" and "the new life which begins within us." To Schelling, writing in 1804, the consummation of philosophy will be a "golden age, of an eternal peace"; this is to be reached, however, not by "external activity" but by a cognitive turnaround, back to the lost "inner identity with the Absolute" which "will be the true revolution [*Revolution*], the idea of which is utterly different from that which has been called by that name."

Kant's "philosophical chiliasm" has its literary parallel in the imaginative chiliasm espoused by Romantic writers in verse and prose. In *The Prelude* Wordsworth narrates the spiritual crisis consequent on the failure of his revolutionary millenarianism, followed by his recovery and a recognition of his mature identity which is also the discovery of his poetic vocation. Attendant upon this discovery is his vision of the world transformed by imagination, which it is his poetic mission to make public:

> And I remember well
> That in life's every-day appearances
> I seemed about this period to have sight
> Of a new world—a world, too, that was fit
> To be transmitted and made visible
> To other eyes—

a new world which is to be achieved, not by political activity, but by an "ennobling interchange / Of action from within and from without" (12.368–71). A similar new world, brought about by a spiritual revolution which yields an apocalypse of imagination, is the end state in many other Romantic writings, whether in the form of autobiography, epic, prose romance, or drama. These include Blake's prophetic poems, Shelley's *Prometheus Unbound* and other visionary works, Carlyle's *Sartor Resartus*, Hölderlin's *Hyperion*, as well as Novalis's *Heinrich von Ofterdingen* and the literary genre he called the *Märchen*, with its fusion of classical, scientific, occult, and especially eschatological elements. What Novalis says in his cryptic notes on the *Märchen* is relevant to the vatic literary works of his age. "It is at the end the primal world, the golden age." But this end is to be achieved by "Man" himself as "the Messiah of nature," and the event is told in the form of a "New Testament—and new nature—as New Jerusalem." In *Sartor Resartus* Carlyle echoes Novalis on man as "the Messias of Nature," and his Teufelsdröckh says that, after his agonized mental crisis, he "awoke to a new Heaven and a new Earth"; this, however, was the old earth, seen anew because "my mind's eyes were now unsealed." And he exhorts the reader that if his "eyesight" were to become "unsealed," he would also see "that this fair Universe, were it in the meanest province thereof, is in very deed the star-domed City of God." In the early 1830s Carlyle thus summarized the endeavor of the preceding generation to achieve a New Jerusalem not by changing the world, but by changing the way we see the world, through an exchange of what he calls the "Imaginative" faculty for the "Understanding" and the merely physical eye.

The Seer and the Bard

Throughout the altering interpretations and applications of the apocalyptic theme, a persistent element is the interpreter's representation of himself as a philosopher-seer or poet-prophet—in the British version, a "Bard"—in the lineage of the biblical prophets of apocalypse. At the height of his millenarian expectations in 1641, Milton had celebrated the coming of "the Eternal and shortly-expected King" to proclaim "thy universal and milde Monarchy through Heaven and Earth." At that time "some one" (patently Milton himself)

> may perhaps bee heard offering at high *strains* in new and lofty *Measures* to sing and celebrate thy . . . *marvelous Judgments* in this Land throughout all ages.
>
> (*Of Reformation*)

Two centuries later, in *The Ages of the World* (1811), Schelling announced the approaching culmination of philosophy in a renewal of the primordial union between mind and nature which will effect a paradisal world: "There will be one world, and the peace of the golden age will make itself known for the first time in the harmonious union of all sciences." Like Milton, Schelling (who had himself once undertaken an epic poem) heralds the seer who will chant this ultimate state of consciousness:

> Perhaps he will yet come who is to sing the greatest heroic poem, comprehending in spirit what was, what is, what will be, the kind of poem attributed to the seers of yore.

Hegel in his *Phenomenology of Spirit* (1807) had already assumed the office of a seer who, as the qualified spokesman for, as well as participant in, the Spirit is able to recapitulate its long evolution in human consciousness and history; in the final paragraph he represents the consummation of the Spirit's development in "Absolute Knowing" as an event that takes place in the consciousness of Hegel himself, in the very act of writing that conclusion. Schelling's seer who comprehends "what was, what is, what will be" coincides exactly with Blake's prophetic persona as "the Bard! / Who Present, Past & Future, sees." This role is assumed also by Novalis, as well as by Carlyle, who is the transitional figure between the Romantic seer and the Victorian prophet. In the original introduction to the "Prospectus" for his high poetic argument, Wordsworth claims that he has been granted "an internal brightness" that "is shared by none," which both qualifies and compels him, "divinely taught," to speak "of what in man is human and divine." He proceeds to announce the paradise which will be regained by the wedding of mind to nature, and his office as the poet-prophet who

> long before the blissful hour arrives,
> Would chant in lonely peace the spousal verse
> Of this great consummation.

Hölderlin had also assumed the stance of elected prophet in his odes of the early 1790s which proclaimed that "zur Vollendung geht die Menschheit ein," and again, late in the 1790s, in the visionary passages of his prose *Hyperion*.

More than two decades later Shelley announced, in the final chorus of *Hellas* (1821),

> The world's great age begins anew
> The golden years return.

In a note appended to this chorus Shelley reveals that, in the course of his poetic life, he has become a touch ironic about assuming the role of "bard," and much less assured about the validity of bardic prophecy. But with that combination of empirical skepticism and indefeasible idealism characteristic of his poetic maturity, Shelley pleads as his exemplars Isaiah, the Old Testament prophet of an enduring earthly millennium, and Virgil, whose "messianic" fourth eclogue, interpreted as an approximation to revealed truth, had over the Christian centuries motivated the conflation of the return of the pagan golden age with the recovery of paradise prophesied in Revelation:

> To anticipate however darkly a period of regeneration and happiness is a . . . hazardous exercise of the faculty which bards possess or feign. It will remind the reader . . . of Isaiah and Virgil, whose ardent spirits overleaping the actual reign of evil which we endure and bewail, already saw the possible and perhaps approaching state of society in which the *"lion shall lie down with the lamb,"* and "omnis feret omnia tellus." Let these great names be my authority and my excuse.

The Judaeo-Christian Apocalypse

John R. May

Both Judaism and Christianity developed myths of future catastrophe, of an end that would come only once in the history of the world. The apocalyptic literature that appeared late in Judaism reached its perfection in the last book of the Christian canon. The end will come only once because, in the Judaeo-Christian worldview, time is linear and irreversible. Not that there are not suggestions of the cyclic in the pattern of its liturgy and in the "return to innocence" that is implicit in the *metanoia* urged upon the individual; these analogies to primitive cult are indeed there. But time is not cyclic, and this is the uniqueness of Judaeo-Christianity in the perspective of world religions. It has accepted the irreversibility of time, the terror of history. It sees the value of the historical hour for salvation. Moreover, since the Incarnation of Christ took place in history, history has shown itself capable of sustaining hierophany in a much more profound sense even than God's revelation of himself to the Hebrew people in the events of the covenant. In the Incarnation, according to Christian belief, God himself became event for man in history. So any Judaeo-Christian expectation of an end to the world would obviously have to come *in* history, even if it would mean the end of time and of history.

According to R. H. Charles, Hebrew apocalypse made a substantial contribution to the religious thought of Israel, and so to the religious thought of man. And in so doing it advanced considerably beyond the richest thought of the prophets of Israel. It professed belief, in its maturest

From *Toward a New Earth: Apocalypse in the American Novel.* © 1972 by the University of Notre Dame Press.

form, in a catastrophic end to the present world, with the expectation of a "new heaven and a new earth" as the work of God extended beyond the fold of Israel to all men as individuals, whereas the noblest expectation of the prophets had confined itself to Israel as a nation. And, in both Judaism and Christianity, there is belief that the end of the world will be preceded by a series of cosmic and historical calamities that will act as its announcement—famines, droughts, wars, the appearance of the Antichrist, celestial signs, and so forth. [Mircea] Eliade puts these signs preceding the end in mythical perspective by pointing out that they are evidence of "the traditional motif of extreme decadence, of the triumph of evil and darkness, which precede the change of aeon and the renewal of the cosmos" (*Cosmos and History*).

The most significant aspect of Old Testament apocalypse, though, would seem to be in the area of its unlimited view of history, its acceptance of the totality of history as it had accepted the totality of the human race. And thus it distinguished itself again from even the best of the prophetic literature. Prophecy dealt only incidentally with the past, concerned as it was with the present and the future and the organic relationship between the two; whereas apocalypse strove to show how past, present, and future were woven together into a single unity. Apocalyptic literature was interested in the future as the solution to the past and the present; but it also sought, in Charles's words, "to get behind the surface and penetrate to the essence of events, the spiritual purposes and forces that underlie and give them their real significance. With this end in view apocalyptic sketched in outline the history of the world and of mankind, the origin of evil, its course, and inevitable overthrow, the ultimate triumph of righteousness, and the final consummation of all things." The total view of history hopefully affords sufficient distance from the crisis at hand to permit the believer to discover God's will for the present as well as the overall meaning of human existence.

There are two eminent commentators on Israel's apocalyptic tradition whose interpretation is so divergent from the one taken here that they must certainly be heard; they are Gerhard von Rad and Martin Buber. It is precisely because of the general nature of the overview of history sketched above that von Rad faults Hebrew apocalypse for being "devoid of theology" (*Old Testament Theology*). It knows nothing, he asserts, of those saving acts of God in history that the theology of the prophets was rooted in. Von Rad, moreover, agrees with Martin Buber about the determinism of Old Testament apocalypse. Its eschatological and transcendental dualism, von Rad claims, clearly differentiates between the present and the future aeon; and the future is "already pre-existent in the world above and come[s] down from there to earth." Martin Buber focuses on the predictive content of apocalypse and sees the clear resolution of the conflict between good and evil in God's favor as an indication of the radical determinism of apocalyptic writing. His thesis is that prophecy, on the other hand, is open-ended concerning the historical hour; its structure is basically dialogical, with God and man working out together the future of the world. Yet even though he admits that the faith inherent in prophecy is the same as for apocalypse, namely, that God will prevail, he insists that prophecy as an expression of the achievement of the human spirit in its relationship with transcendence preserves more tellingly man's freedom insofar as it emphasizes man's capacity to turn either toward or away from God.

Apocalypse, says Buber, overlooks history and man's capacity for shaping it in favor of the consummation to be received from outside of history: "The mature apocalyptic, moreover, no longer knows an historical future in the real sense. The end of all history is near. . . . The proper and paradoxical subject of the late apocalyptic is a future that is no longer in time, and he anticipates this consummation so that for him all that may yet come in history no longer has an historical character. Man cannot achieve this future, but he also has nothing more to achieve." On the other hand, Buber continues, prophecy does not fix the future because its understanding of the transcendent is of a God who wants man to turn to him with full freedom out of his hopelessness. Buber insists that this is the prophetic *theologem,* although he admits that it is "never expressed as such but firmly embedded in the foundations of Hebrew prophecy."

Taking an overall view of his treatment of the distinction between prophecy and apocalypse, one wishes that Buber had been as generous in selecting material from apocalypse as he was in determining the nature of prophecy. He has, for example, simply ignored all of messianic prophecy and the content of its inspired word—which gets to be quite specific, almost deterministic, as far as the nation is concerned—in favor of the dialogical reciprocity that he finds in Jeremiah's debate with God. In *Pointing the Way,* he concentrates upon the Fourth Book of Ezra for his analysis of the meaning of apocalypse. His scholarly concern does not extend to the New Testament Book of Revelation, where a dialogical framework is indeed implicit in the letters to the churches. Moreover, the Book of Revelation is aware of God's saving act in Jesus; this is actually its pervasive concern. Von Rad's argument, therefore, about the lack of theological perspective in Old Testament apocalypse obviously could not be leveled against the Book of Revelation. And, as William Beardslee observes, the determinism of apocalyptic literature, "as in Calvinism, is an expression of wonder at the glory of God." The present crisis is so distressing that the believer knows he can be saved only by God. Buber and von Rad notwithstanding, it is certainly a respectable scholarly approach to the relationship between prophecy and apocalypse to see them not as diametrically opposed, with apocalypse representing the disintegration of a tradition, but rather, following Charles and other standard commentators, as stages in a developing understanding of faith.

Few modern commentators on the literature of apocalypse, specifically on its most developed expression in the New Testament, will stress or even mention what Buber and von Rad object to as the otherworldly aspect of apocalyptic literature, of a consummation coming from God outside of history. N. Turner, for example, in *Peake's Commentary on the Bible,* says that the Book of Revelation is "much more concerned with the course of world-history than with the fate of souls after death." H. H. Rowley sees Revelation as having at least this in common with the rest of apocalyptic literature, that it expresses faith in a God who is directing the course of human history according to a plan that he intends to see through to completion; and this decidedly includes his victory over evil. Andre Feuillet, a Catholic commentator, feels that Revelation gives a Christian meaning to history by inveighing against the easy optimism of imminent victory; and in presenting life as an enduring struggle that will eventually be won by Christ, Revelation offers us a "theological datum" rather than a chronological observation. Feuillet, considering the theological implications of the titles attributed to Jesus, judges the book to possess one of the most developed Christologies of the New Testament. Like the Epistle to the Hebrews, he notes, it counsels perseverance amid stress. In relation to the Old Testament, and thus to the expanded interest in human history that Charles noted, Revelation shows how the true meaning of history, going all the way back to Genesis, becomes clear only in Christ.

If apocalypse is not primarily concerned with another world, what is it concerned with? An attempt to redefine apocalypse could obviously appear to be just another word game, or an evasion of what everyone accepts as true. For even though Turner can insist that the apocalyptic style developed "in periods of stress to encourage readers to persevere in faith and good works," a traditionalist understanding would jump immediately to the conclusion that the obvious reason why Christians are to persevere under trial is that their true home is not really of this world.

I suggest that the import of apocalypse as it developed in the Hebrew and Christian canons had nothing to do with holding the carrot of eternity before the believer's nose. It is true that history is seen as a mystery of God's planning, a mystery that will ultimately be revealed as his victory over the perversity of human freedom; but the precise raison d'être for apocalypse is to deny the imminence of easy victory, to force Jews and Christians alike to accept the agony of history, the birth pangs of creation. My emphasis here on the theme of denial of imminent victory does not derogate from the obvious apocalyptic concentration on the end. The desire for "total presence" that Beardslee sees embodied in apocalyptic form is necessitated paradoxically, as he notes, by "the threat of a total victory of evil." Feuillet proposes that the basic teaching of Revelation, a viewpoint common to the whole New Testament, is that "Christians are now assisting at the painful but guaranteed birth-pangs of the definitive era of final salvation." Elsewhere Feuillet writes: "The Apocalypse does not at all seek to soothe its readers by dulling illusions of peace; rather, the author shows the life of the Church as endlessly plagued by terrible crimes of every kind, bringing thereby a needed counterbalance to the naive and unjustified self-deception that progress is automatic and imminent for the Church."

The rejection of naive optimism and the denial of imminent victory is the message confirmed by the very structure of the Book of Revelation, and this type of consideration is obviously germane to our analysis of literary apocalypse. Its progressively expanding rhythm of sevens, each of which creates the illusion of a complete vision only to explode into a subsequent vision of seven, continually shatters the mood of expectation that the author seemed so carefully to be creating. Each of the six weeks of seven days, as Austin Farrer has demonstrated so capably, each successive series of visions, is intended to create and shatter the illusion of imminent completion of the apocalypse. Thus, the total effect of the ever-retreating horizon of fulfillment is to support a mood of genuine hope amid frustration.

The place of Revelation in the New Testament canon, obviously crucial for understanding its meaning, is analogous to the position of apocalyptic literature in the Old Testament. For the development of apocalypse late in the Old Testament period was undoubtedly a response to unfulfilled prophecy, just as Revelation marked faith's rejection of the illusion of imminent surcease that had been created by the advent of the Messiah (an illusion that is very much in evidence in the earlier New Testament writings). The closer man comes to God, the more tangible his revelation, the greater the human temptation to expect immediate deliverance from the terror of existence. Revelation, therefore, represents the most mature reflection of the New Testament faith. Expressed in poetic language, though, it has often eluded the grasp of a church plagued by the logic of scholasticism.

Apocalypse is a response to cultural crisis. It grows out of that sense of loss that results from the passing of an old worldview. Of all of the recent analysts of apocalypse, no one has expressed this more precisely than Amos Wilder [in a paper read before the American Academy of Religion, 1970]:

> Common to all true apocalyptic is a situation characterized by anomie, a loss of "world," or erosion of structures, psychic and cultural, with the consequent nakedness to Being or immediacy to the Mystery. Hence the rhetorics of this "panic" exposure in which existence itself is at stake, involving antinomies of life and death, light and darkness, knowledge and nescience, order and chaos. And it can never be only a question of the individual. It is a juncture which renews the archaic crisis of all existence, that of survival, the viability of life, the viability of the human. Since inherited structures and mediacies of a dependable order are forfeit, the only available dramatizations of the crisis and of any projected "future" will necessarily have a pre-cultural character. Pre-cultural, first in a temporal sense: a return to archaic motifs and to deeply buried hierophanies of the community. But pre-cultural also in the sense of a language responsive to the unmediated dynamics that underlie all Being and Becoming.

In the Book of Revelation, loss of world takes the form of the imagined darkness attendant upon the rejected expectation of an imminent establishment of God's final kingdom; mature faith accepts the enduring struggle that historical existence entails. In contemporary literature, loss of world expresses itself in the same arcane images, the precultural images of conflict and destruction that Amos Wilder describes, yet frequently without the sense of continuity that existed through the period of normative Christian apocalypse. One obvious reason for this would seem to be the loss of faith that allows one to project a future. Cultural turmoil is reflected in the breakdown of the language tradition that holds together man's view of the world; yet throughout the agonizing passage to another linguistic expression of faith, the reality of faith must apparently remain, though inarticulate, if man is to bridge the cultural chasm with hope.

Apocalypse, of all the New Testament literary forms, expresses clear awareness of man's painful "fall into history," a phrase of Mircea Eliade's that captures perfectly the realization underlying apocalyptic vision. The full implication of living in history, of the ravages of conditioned human existence, is what is intended by this expression. The very place of salvation is now an obstacle to salvation. The very event in which God comes to man must be sought in the obscurity of history. When the sacred manifested itself only in the cosmos, it was fairly easy to recognize, particularly when an object was charged with power or when through the repetition of a ritual sacred time began again. The Christian, though, "has continually to *choose,* to try to distinguish, in the tangle of historical events, the event which, *for him,* may be charged with a saving significance" (Eliade, *Myths, Dreams, and Mysteries*). The day-to-day agony of discernment is the result of Christian acceptance of the fall into history, and it is this realization that the display of violent images in Revelation gives witness to. Christians thus spare themselves at least the futile agony of discerning the end. They accept, and even yearn for, the end as fulfillment of a promise, God's promise of fidelity, but in the meantime turn their full attention to the ambiguous face of history.

A clear purpose of the Book of Revelation, then, is to aid the experience of mature faith, the acceptance of a call to work out one's salvation in the ambiguity of irreversible time. Final salvation is not at hand; in fact, the experience of faith is an acceptance of hope that makes no demands. One cannot escape history by thinking that the work is over or that it will be ended shortly. If one expects an imminent end, Revelation teaches, his hope is indeed vain—and his faith patently immature.

Although there is certainly no need to enter into the debate about the author of Revelation, whether he was John the apostle or some other well-known John, I must nonetheless point out that the continuing dispute over authorship opens up the possibility that the New Testament apocalypse was written pseudonymously as all Jewish apocalypses after 200 B.C. undoubtedly were—and of necessity, as R. H. Charles has shown. Apocalypse in the Old Testament dates from the period in Judaism when the law was everything, and the only way the writers could proclaim their very urgent message concerning the genuine eschatological thrust of their faith over the din of legalism was to give their work the sanctity of tradition. The author of Revelation perhaps chose the name of one of the sons of thunder because he wanted that association to add weight to his words of judgment against those who would codify their faith in Christ into easy optimism. John had asked to share the chalice and did no doubt in a measure beyond his expectation, and, says the author of Revelation, so would anyone who calls himself a follower of Christ.

The very medium of Christian faith *is* hope, Jürgen Moltmann has reminded us: "The eschatological is not one element *of* Christianity, but it is the medium of Christian faith as such, the key in which everything in it is set, the glow that suffuses everything here in the dawn of an expected new day." It is a medium though without historical specification, without perhaps any other content than the one demonstrated by the author of Revelation; namely that God *will* fulfill his promises. The emphasis in Revelation is on the future, but in such a way that belief in the fulfillment of the promise can enlighten one's acceptance of the past and strengthen his approach to the present. Hope alone can illumine the future.

Apocalyptic literature, moreover, uses the mythic framework of the regeneration of the world as a macrocosmic idiom for another important Christian concern, the *metanoia* of the individual. The author of Revelation is certainly conscious of the fact that he addresses the individual hearer within the context of his church. "Hear, you who have ears to hear, what the Spirit says to the Churches!" (Rev. 2:7). Christian metanoia is always a turning toward God by turning to the neighbor; so when we speak of the regeneration of the individual, our frame of theological reference is not merely vertical. The regeneration that is promised to the world is offered to the hearer now if he will turn from his former evil ways and accept as reality the possibility of starting anew in response to the word spoken to him. Judgment is leveled against the churches within the imaginative context of cosmic judgment, and the norm that is offered in support of judgment is the expected righteousness of Christ. Thus the imagery of conflict found in Revelation sharpens the call to repentance, most specifically for the sin of presumption.

The image of the eternal city which concludes the vision of Revelation is a perfect complement to the paradisiacal myth of Genesis. Men fail in righteousness when they turn away from the daily agony of building up the city of man. The myth of paradise, naive and primitive as a statement of man's origin, becomes reasonable eschatological expectation at the end of the Book of Revelation, a more mature expression of religious belief when viewed as the destiny man gropes toward in the darkness of the future. The exemplary pattern of behavior is no longer what the gods did *in illo tempore,* but the promised city of light and love that Christians are in agony to bring forth.

Apocalypse

D. H. Lawrence

When we come to the second half of Revelation, after the newborn child is snatched to heaven and the woman has fled into the wilderness, there is a sudden change, and we feel we are reading purely Jewish and Jewish Christian Apocalypse, with none of the old background.

"And there was war in heaven: Michael and his angels fought against the dragon."—They cast down the dragon out of heaven into the earth, and he becomes Satan, and ceases entirely to be interesting. When the great figures of mythology are turned into rationalised or merely moral forces, then they lose interest. We are acutely bored by moral angels and moral devils. We are acutely bored by a "rationalised" Aphrodite. Soon after 1000 B.C. the world went a little insane about morals and "sin." The Jews had always been tainted.

What we have been looking for in the Apocalypse is something older, grander than the ethical business. The old, flaming love of life and the strange shudder of the presence of the invisible dead made the rhythm of really ancient religion. Moral religion is comparatively modern, even with the Jews.

But the second half of the Apocalypse is all moral: that is to say, it is all sin and salvation. For a moment there is a hint of the old cosmic wonder, when the dragon turns again upon the woman, and she is given wings of an eagle and flies off into the wilderness: but the dragon pursues her and spues out a flood upon her, to overwhelm her: "and the earth helped the woman, and the earth opened her mouth and swallowed up

---

From *Apocalypse,* edited by Mara Kalnins. © 1931 by the Estate of David Herbert Lawrence, © 1980 by the Estate of Frieda Lawrence Ravagli. Viking, 1982.

the flood. And the dragon was wroth with the woman, and went to make war on the remnant of her seed, *which keep the commandments of God, and have the testimony of Jesus Christ.*"

The last words are, of course, the moral ending tacked on by some Jew-Christian scribe to the fragment of myth. The dragon is here the watery dragon, or the dragon of chaos, and in his evil aspect still. He is resisting with all his might the birth of a new thing, a new era. He turns against the Christians, since they are the only "good" thing left on earth.

The poor dragon henceforth cuts a sorry figure. He gives his power, and his seat, and great authority to the beast that rises out of the sea, the beast with "seven heads and ten horns and upon his head ten crowns, and upon his heads the name of blasphemy. And the beast which I saw was like unto a leopard, and his feet were as the feet of a bear, and his mouth as the mouth of a lion"—

We know this beast already: he comes out of Daniel and is *explained* by Daniel. The beast is the last grand world-empire, the ten horns are ten kingdoms confederated in the empire—which is of course Rome. As for the leopard, bear and lion qualities, these are also explained in Daniel as the three empires that preceded Rome, the Macedonian, swift as a leopard, the Persian, stubborn as a bear, the Babylonian, rapacious as the lion.

We are back again at the level of allegory, and for me, the real interest is gone. Allegory can always be explained: and explained away. The true symbol defies all explanation, so does the true myth. You can give meanings to either—you will never explain them away. Because symbol and myth do not affect us only mentally, they move the deep emotional centres every time. The great quality of the mind is finality. The mind "understands," and there's an end of it.

But the emotional consciousness of man has a life and movement quite different from the mental consciousness. The mind knows in part, in part and parcel, with full stop after every sentence. But the emotional soul knows in full, like a river or a flood. For example, the symbol of the dragon—look at it, on a Chinese teacup or in an old woodcut, read it in a fairy tale—and what is the result? If you are alive in the old emotional self, the more you look at the dragon, and think of it, the farther and farther flushes out your emotional awareness, on and on into dim regions of the soul aeons and aeons back. But if you are dead in the old feeling-knowing way, as so many moderns are, then the dragon just "stands for" this that and the other—all the things it stands for in Frazer's *Golden Bough*: it is just a kind of glyph or label, like the gilt pestle and mortar outside a chemist's shop.—Or take better still the Egyptian symbol called the *ankh*, the symbol of life etc.   which the goddesses hold in their hands. Any child "knows what it means." But a man who is *really* alive feels his soul begin to throb and expand at the mere sight of the symbol. Modern men, however, are nearly all half-dead, modern women too. So they just look at the ankh and know all about it, and that's that. They are proud of their own emotional impotence.

Naturally, then, the Apocalypse has appealed to men through the ages as an "allegorical" work. Everything just "meant something"—and something moral at that. You can put down the meaning flat.

The beast from the sea means Roman Empire—and later Nero, number 666. The beast from the earth means the pagan sacerdotal power, the priestly power which made the emperors divine and made Christians even "worship" them. For the beast from the earth has two horns like a lamb, a false Lamb indeed, an Antichrist, and it teaches its wicked followers to perform marvels and even miracles—of witchcraft, like Simon Magus and the rest.

So we have the Church of Christ—or of the Messiah—being martyred by the beast, till pretty well all good Christians are martyred. Then at last, after not so very long a time—say forty years—the Messiah descends from heaven and makes war on the beast, the Roman Empire, and on the kings who are with him. There is a grand fall of Rome, called Babylon, and a grand triumph over her downfall—though the best poetry is all the time lifted from Jeremiah or Ezekiel or Isaiah, it is not original. The sainted Christians gloat over fallen Rome: and then the Victorious Rider appears, his shirt bloody with the blood of dead kings. After this, a New Jerusalem descends to be his Bride, and these precious martyrs all get their thrones, and for a thousand years (John was not going to be put off with Enoch's meagre forty) for a thousand years, the grand Millennium, the Lamb reigns over the earth, assisted by all the risen martyrs. And if the martyrs in the Millennium are going to be as bloodthirsty and ferocious as John the Divine in the Apocalypse—Revenge Timotheus cries—then somebody's going to get it hot during the thousand years of the rule of saints.

But this is not enough. After the thousand years the whole universe must be wiped out, earth, sun, moon, stars and sea. These early Christians fairly lusted after the end of the world. They wanted their own grand turn first—Revenge Timotheus cries!—But after that, they insisted that the whole universe must be wiped out, sun, stars and all—and a *new* New Jerusalem should appear, with the same old saints and martyrs in glory, and everything else should have disappeared except the lake of burning brimstone in which devils, demons, beasts and bad men should frizzle and suffer for ever and ever and ever, Amen!

So ends this glorious work: surely a rather repulsive work. Revenge was indeed a sacred duty to the Jerusalem Jews: and it is not the revenge one minds so much as the perpetual self-glorification of these saints and martyrs, and their profound impudence. How one loathes them, in their "new white garments." How disgusting their priggish rule must be! How vile is their spirit, really, insisting, simply insisting on wiping out the whole universe, bird and blossom, star and river, and above all, everybody except *themselves* and their precious "saved" brothers. How beastly their new Jerusalem, where the flowers never fade, but stand in everlasting sameness! How terribly bourgeois to have unfading flowers!

No wonder the pagans were horrified at the "impious" Christian desire to destroy the universe. How horrified even the old Jews of the Old Testament would have been. For even to them, earth and sun and stars were eternal, created in the grand creation by Almighty God. But no, these impudent martyrs must see it all go up in smoke.

Oh, it is the Christianity of the middling masses, this Christianity of the Apocalypse. And we must confess, it is hideous. Self-righteousness, self-conceit, self-importance, and secret *envy* underlie it all.

By the time of Jesus, all the lowest classes and mediocre people had realised that *never* would they get a chance to be kings, *never* would they go in chariots, never would they drink wine from gold vessels. Very well then—they would have their revenge by *destroying* it all. "Babylon the great is fallen, is fallen, and is become the habitation of devils." And then all the gold and silver and pearls and precious stones and fine linen and purple, and silk, and scarlet—and cinnamon and frankincense, wheat, beasts, sheep, horses, chariots, slaves, souls of men—all these that are destroyed, destroyed, destroyed in Babylon the great—! how one hears the envy, the endless envy screeching through this song of triumph!

No, we can understand that the Fathers of the Church in the East wanted Apocalypse left out of the New Testament. But like Judas among the disciples, it was inevitable that it should be included. The Apocalypse is the feet of clay to the grand Christian image. And down crashes the image, on the weakness of these very feet.

There is Jesus—but there is also John the Divine. There is Christian love—and there is Christian envy. The former would "save" the world—the latter will never be satisfied till it has destroyed the world. They are two sides of the same medal.

Because, as a matter of fact, when you start to teach individual self-realisation to the great masses of people, who when all is said and done are only *fragmentary* beings, *incapable* of whole individuality, you end by making them all envious, grudging, spiteful creatures. Anyone who is kind to man knows the fragmentariness of most men, and wants to arrange a society of power in which men fall naturally into a collective wholeness, since they *cannot* have an individual wholeness. In this collective wholeness they will be fulfilled. But if they make efforts at individual fulfilment, they *must* fail, for they are by nature fragmentary. Then, failures, having no wholeness anywhere, they fall into envy and spite. Jesus knew all about it when he said: "To them that have shall be given" etc.—But he had forgotten to reckon with the mass of the mediocre, whose motto is: we have nothing and therefore nobody shall have anything!

But Jesus gave the ideal for the Christian individual, and deliberately avoided giving an ideal for the state or the nation. When he said "Render unto Caesar that which is Caesar's," he left to Caesar the rule of men's bodies, willy-nilly: and this threatened terrible danger to a man's mind and soul. Already by the year 60 A.D. the Christians were an accursed sect; and they were compelled, like all men, to sacrifice, that is, to give worship to the living Caesar. In giving Caesar the power over men's bodies, Jesus gave him the power to compel men to make the act of worship to Caesar. Now I doubt if Jesus himself could have performed this act of worship, to a Nero or a Domitian. No doubt he would have preferred death. As did so many early Christian martyrs. So there, at the very beginning, was a monstrous dilemma. To be a Christian meant death at the hands of the Roman State; since to submit to the cult of the Emperor and worship the divine man, Caesar, was impossible to a Christian. No wonder, then, that John of Patmos saw the day not far off when *every* Christian would be martyred. The day would have come, if the imperial cult had been absolutely enforced on the people. And then when *every* Christian was martyred, what could a Christian expect but a Second Advent, resurrection, and an absolute revenge! There was a condition for the Christian community to be in, sixty years after the death of the Saviour.

Jesus made it inevitable, when he said that the money belonged to Caesar. It was a mistake. Money means bread, and the bread of men belongs to no man. Money means also power, and it is monstrous to give power to the virtual enemy. Caesar was *bound,* sooner or later, to violate the soul of the Christians. But Jesus saw the individual only, and considered only the individual. He left it to John of Patmos, who was up against the Roman State, to formulate the Christian vision of the Christian State. John did it in the Apocalypse. It entails the destruction of the whole world, and the reign of saints in ultimate bodiless glory. Or it entails the destruction of all earthly power, and the rule of an oligarchy of martyrs (the Millennium).

This destruction of all earthly power we are now moving towards. The oligarchy of martyrs began with Lenin, and apparently Mussolini is also a martyr. Strange, strange people they are, the martyrs, with weird cold morality. When every country has its martyr-ruler, either like Lenin or like Mussolini, what a strange, unthinkable world it will be! But it is coming: the Apocalypse is still a book to conjure with.

A few vastly important points have been missed by Christian doctrine and Christian thought. Christian fantasy alone has grasped them.

1. No man is or can be a pure individual. The mass of men have only the tiniest touch of individuality: if any. The mass of men live and move, think and feel collectively, and have practically no individual emotions, feelings or thoughts at all. They are fragments of the collective or social consciousness. It has always been so, and will always be so.

2. The State, or what we call Society as a collective whole *cannot* have the psychology of an individual. Also it is a mistake to say that the State is made up of individuals. It is not. It is made up of a collection of fragmentary beings. And *no* collective act, even so private an act as voting, is made from the individual self. It is made from the collective self, and has another psychological background, nonindividual.

3. The State *cannot* be Christian. Every State is a Power. It cannot be otherwise. Every State must guard its own boundaries and guard its own prosperity. If it fails to do so, it betrays all its individual citizens.

4. Every *citizen* is a unit of worldly power. A *man* may wish to be a pure Christian and a pure individual. But since he *must* be a member of some political State, or Nation, he is forced to be a unit of worldly power.

5. As a citizen, as a collective being, man has his fulfilment in the gratification of his power-sense. If he belongs to one of the so-called "ruling nations," his soul is fulfilled in the sense of his country's power or strength. If his country mounts up aristocratically to a zenith of splendour and power, in a hierarchy, he will be all the more fulfilled, having his place in the hierarchy. But if his country is powerful and democratic, then he will be obsessed with a perpetual will to assert his power in

interfering and *preventing* other people from doing as they wish, since no man must do more than another man. This is the condition of modern democracies, a condition of perpetual bullying.

In democracy, bullying inevitably takes the place of power. Bullying is the negative form of power. The modern Christian State is a soul-destroying force, for it is made up of fragments which have no organic whole, only a collective whole. In a hierarchy, each part is organic and vital, as my finger is an organic and vital part of me. But a democracy is bound in the end to be obscene, for it is composed of myriad disunited fragments, each fragment assuming to itself a false wholeness, a false individuality. Modern democracy is made up of millions of frictional parts all asserting their own wholeness.

6. To have an ideal for the individual which regards only his individual self and ignores his collective self is in the long run fatal. To have a creed of individuality which denies the reality of the hierarchy makes at last for mere anarchy. Democratic man lives by cohesion and resistance, the cohesive force of "love" and the resistant force of the individual "freedom." To yield entirely to love would be to be absorbed, which is the death of the individual: for the individual must hold his own, or he ceases to be "free" and individual. So that we see, what our age has proved to its astonishment and dismay, that the individual *cannot* love. The individual cannot love: let that be an axiom. And the modern man or woman *cannot* conceive of himself, herself, save as an individual. And the individual in man or woman is *bound* to kill, at last, the lover in himself, or herself. It is not that each man kills the thing he loves, but that each man, by insisting on his own individuality, kills the lover in himself, as the woman kills the lover in herself. The Christian *dare not love*: for love kills that which is Christian, democratic and modern, the individual. The individual *cannot* love. When the individual loves, he ceases to be purely individual. And so he *must* recover himself, and cease to love. It is one of the most amazing lessons of our day: that the individual, the Christian, the democrat *cannot* love. Or, when he loves, when she loves, he *must* take it back, she *must* take it back.

So much for private or personal love. Then what about that other love, "caritas," loving your neighbour as yourself?

It works out the same. You love your neighbour. Immediately you run the risk of being absorbed by him: you must draw back, you must hold your own. The love becomes resistance. In the end, it is all resistance and no love: which is the history of democracy.

If you are taking the path of individual self-realisation, you had better, like Buddha, go off and be by yourself, and give a thought to nobody. Then you may achieve your Nirvana. Christ's way of loving your neighbour leads to the hideous anomaly of having to live by sheer resistance to your neighbour, in the end.

The Apocalypse, strange book, makes this clear. It shows us the Christian in his relation to the State: which the Gospels and Epistles avoid doing. It shows us the Christian in relation to the State, to the world, and to the cosmos. It shows him in mad hostility to all of them, having, in the end, to will the destruction of them all.

It is the dark side of Christianity, of individualism, and of democracy, the side the world at large now shows us. And it is, simply, suicide. Suicide individual and en masse. If man could will it, it would be cosmic suicide. But the cosmos is not at man's mercy, and the sun will not perish to please us.

We do not want to perish, either. We have to give up a false position. Let us give up our false position as Christians, as individuals, and as democrats. Let us find some conception of ourselves that will allow us to be peaceful and happy, instead of tormented and unhappy.

The Apocalypse shows us what we are resisting, unnaturally. We are unnaturally resisting our connection with the cosmos, with the world, with mankind, with the nation, with the family. All these connections are, in the Apocalypse, anathema, and they are anathema to us. We *cannot bear connection*. That is our malady. We *must* break away, and be isolate. We call that being free, being individual. Beyond a certain point, which we have reached, it is suicide. Perhaps we have chosen suicide. Well and good. The Apocalypse too chose suicide, with subsequent self-glorification.

But the Apocalypse shows, by its very resistance, the things that the human heart secretly yearns after. By the very frenzy with which the Apocalypse destroys the sun and the stars, the world, and all kings and all rulers, all scarlet and purple and cinnamon, all harlots, finally all men altogether who are not "sealed," we can see how deeply the apocalyptists are yearning for the sun and the stars and the earth and the waters of the earth, for nobility and lordship and might, and scarlet and gold, splendour, for passionate love, and a proper unison with men, apart from this sealing business. What man most passionately wants is his living wholeness and his living unison, not his own isolate salvation of his "soul." Man wants his physical fulfilment first and foremost, since now, once and once only, he is in the flesh and potent. For man, the vast marvel is to be alive. For man, as for flower and beast and bird, the supreme triumph is to be most vividly, most perfectly alive. Whatever the unborn and the dead may know, they cannot know the beauty, the marvel of being alive in the flesh. The dead may look after the afterwards. But the magnificent here and now of life in the flesh is ours, and ours alone, and ours only for a time. We ought to dance with rapture that we should be alive and in the flesh, and part of the living, incarnate cosmos. I am part of the sun as my eye is part of me. That I am part of the earth my feet know perfectly, and my blood is part of the sea. My soul knows that I am part of the human race, my soul is an organic part of the great human soul, as my spirit is part of my nation. In my own very self, I am part of my family. There is nothing of me that is alone and absolute except my mind, and we shall find that the mind has no existence by itself, it is only the glitter of the sun on the surface of the waters.

So that my individualism is really an illusion. I am a part of the great whole, and I can never escape. But I *can* deny my connections, break them, and become a fragment. Then I am wretched.

What we want is to destroy our false, inorganic connections, especially those related to money, and reestablish the living organic connections, with the cosmos, the sun and earth, with mankind and nation and family. Start with the sun, and the rest will slowly, slowly happen.

A Rebirth of Images:
The Kingdom of Darkness

Austin Farrer

The Kingdom of Darkness is set by St John in elaborate antithesis to the Kingdom of Light. Just as Christ not only expounds the Name of God but is, in his action and his existence, an exposition of the Name, so Antichrist not only blasphemes the Name, he is a living blasphemy of the Name. We have observed [throughout *A Rebirth of Images*] several elements of the demonic parody in the course of running commentary on the text. We will now attempt a more systematic account of it.

We may begin by considering the triad, Dragon, Beast and False Prophet. Of what heavenly triad are they the travesty? We saw St John setting forth the kingdom of God in two triads, the threefold Name and the three divine Persons. It seems fitting that there should be three holy triads, not two; and in fact there is a third. When we were analysing the Trinitarian Blessing in chapter 1 [of Revelation], we found in it a subtle balance between the triad (Father, Son, Spirit) and the dyad (God and Christ). What we have now to add is that this dyad is itself two-thirds of a triad, the three grades of derivation, God, Christ, his Servants. The Spirit and the Name descend in fullness from God to Christ, so that they are his Name and his Spirit. They descend to his servants, also, but not in fullness. The Seal of the Living God is his seal, not theirs, though it marks their foreheads. The brand they bear is Christ's and his Father's Name, not their own. God puts all revelation into the hands of the Son, but it does not descend to the servant save through the ministration of an angel. The complete indwelling of the Father's Spirit in the Son re-

From *A Rebirth of Images: The Making of St. John's Apocalypse.* © 1949, 1963 by Dacre Press. Beacon Press, 1963.

moves all inequality, while it confirms derivation; and so the first two grades are constituted, with the Spirit, a divine Trinity.

We must not ask, "And of what grade is the Spirit?" for that would be to pass outside the form St John is using. The Spirit is precisely the divine Power insofar as he is undetermined to any grade, but passes through them all. If we say, "But we are metaphysicians, and we must have an answer: if the Spirit is an hypostasis of the Godhead, he must have his grade of derivation," we shall, perhaps, be driven to something like the Western Scholastic conclusion: Since he presupposes the generation of the Son into whom he is inbreathed, we must derive him third, the Father sending him and the Son drawing him. But this is to advance into a speculation quite outside St John's forms. He simply sees the Father, with the Spirit beside him as communicable Godhead: and then he sees the two derived grades to which he is communicated, the derived equal, and the derived unequal.

The triad of the grades is, in fact, the triad with which St John begins, inlaying into it the triads of the threefold Name and the three Persons as he proceeds.

> Apocalypse of [2] Jesus Christ, which [1] God gave him, to show [3] his servants what must quickly be,
> and he signified it by the message of his angel to [3] his servant John, who witnessed the word of God [1] and the witness of [2] Jesus Christ in all he saw. . . .
> [3] John to the seven Churches that are in Asia: Grace to you and peace from [1] the IS, WAS and COMETH, and from the Seven Spirits that are before his throne, and from [2] Jesus Christ, the faithful witness.
>
> (Rev. 1:1–5)

As revelation descends from God to Christ, and from Christ to his servants, for example, to John, but to him by the interposition of an angel; so grace and peace proceed *through* the three grades, but *from* the two alone, in whose Name the third blesses. All the saints who hold the word of God and the testimony of Jesus are servants, and partakers of the Spirit, but the inspired man in the act of his inspiration is preeminently or typically so. Then the "servant" becomes "the prophet." St John himself is a prophet, and his book is "this prophecy."

The triad which the demonic figures blaspheme is the triad of derivation. Satan aspires to be a false God, the Beast a false Christ, and the second Beast a false prophet. Satan bestows on Antichrist "his power and his throne, and great authority": the False Prophet "executes all the authority of the first Beast in his sight, and makes the earth . . . to worship the first Beast." In doing so they worship also the Dragon for having bestowed the power upon him. The False Prophet himself is no more worshipped than the Christian prophet is.

Such is the demonic hierarchy, but it is, of course, a sham. There are no real grades in it. The Antichrist and the False Prophet are equally men: the False Prophet is to Antichrist simply what Goebbels was to Hitler (to take the modern example which is least likely to cause ill-feeling), or, as St John implies, what Balaam was to Balak and the magicians to Pharaoh. In being a demon, Satan has no superiority over the other two. Where men worship Satan, the image of God grovels before the serpent. The Satan of the Apocalypse is not the Miltonic archangel with tarnished wings. The Jews of St John's time commonly held a different account of the origin of demons. They were the damned souls of the dead giants, begotten once by the monstrous intercourse of the fallen angels with the daughters of men: the angels themselves had long ago been pinioned to the floor of the abyss. The demons were not what the heathen supposed themselves to be worshipping under the guise of Gods. They aspired to worship the angels of the stars and other parts of nature. But since the worship of the creature is a sin, the demons intercept it, turn it to their own advantage, and work the magic of the heathen cult. Demons are not stronger than men, their power is parasitical on the sin of men. Human error makes the godhead of idols, and human wickedness the sway of demons. Michael could cast down Satan at a blow, if men's sins did not give substance to his accusations in the court of heaven: and the Name of God would everywhere exorcise demonic mischief, if it were everywhere faithfully invoked. Satan is the vast image of a working lie, sprawled across half the heaven, and sweeping off with his tail a third part of the stars.

As there are no real grades of hierarchy in the Kingdom of Darkness, so there is no spirit which passess through them all and knits them into one. There are many demons, no doubt, in the fellowship of Beelzebub, and they will work their tricks in and for the Antichrist and the False Prophet. When the unholy three desire to bring the kings of earth to Armageddon each vomits a demon. These three demons may be felt as a faint parody of "the Seven Spirits of God sent into all the earth," and one of the suggestions contained in the mysterious name of Armageddon supports this line of thought. Ar-mageddon, i.e., Mount Megiddo, is not a name ever used in fact, but if it were, it would presumably describe the Carmel-range; and it was to Carmel that Elijah persuaded Ahab to gather all the prophets of Baal (1 Kings 18:19); and there they contested with God, and met their doom. The spirit of deception which leads the false prophets to assemble against the prophet of God is presumably the vain confidence of their false inspiration, and therefore the spirit which is a parody of the Holy Spirit of true prophecy. Ahab bade the false prophets go to Carmel and perish; they were presently to do the like service for him, when with one voice they exhorted him to go up to Ramoth Gilead, to perish there (1 Kings 22:6) (The Septuagint gives various forms of the name, among others Ramagalaad [2 Chron. 22], Aremoth-Galaad [Josh. 20]. St John may have seen an assonance to such forms in the "Armageddon" which he wrote.). On that occasion Micaiah saw in a vision the lying spirit going forth by divine permission to be a spirit of false prophecy in their mouths: and the mission of this lying spirit is obviously antithetical to that of the Holy Spirit of true inspiration which Micaiah possesses. The false prophets sent the false Anointed to Ramoth Gilead, the false Anointed sent the false prophets to "Mount Megiddo": the false Anointed and the False Prophet each vomit one of the spirits which leads the kings to Armageddon; thither they go themselves too, and there they perish. The third spirit is vomited by the Father of Lies. Ahab is a type of Antichrist in any case, being the husband of Jezebel, who is a type of the Wicked Woman (Rev. 2:20): and the Baal whom they and their prophets worship is, in St John's eyes, no mere type of Satan, he is Satan in person.

We may now consider the figures of the Beasts. Satan is "the Dragon," i.e., Leviathan; he is also "the serpent in the Beginning," the snake which misled Eve, and was doomed to warfare with her seed. The "seed" was to strike his head, and he was to strike the "seed's" heel. Antichrist is "the Beast," i.e., Behemoth; he is also "the seed of the serpent," joined with the serpent in the doom of fruitless war against the woman's seed. This means simply that he is the typical wicked man, the seed of Satan par excellence (see John 8:31ff.).

There is an interchange of features between the Dragon and the Beast. The "stricken head" becomes characteristic of the Beast, though it belongs primarily to the Oracle on the Serpent. The seven heads and ten horns are anticipated in the figure of the Dragon, though they belong properly to Daniel's oracle on the Beast (Dan. 7). Daniel, indeed, distributes the seven heads among four beasts; the great Beast of St John is to be understood as a summing-up (ἀνακεφαλαίωσις) of them all, a quintessence of all the heathen tyrannies of history. The interchange of features between the Dragon and the Antichrist expresses the parody on the relation of the Son to the Father. The Father is mirrored in the Son: the Father's Seven Spirits descend to become the seven horns and eyes of the Lamb.

The heads and horns have in the Dragon no further meaning: they make him simply the archetype of the Beast. (In St John's use of the diagram, however, it is the Dragon who arises out of the place of the Lamb, and so begins naturally enough the parody of his features which afterwards descends to the Beast. In the second Beast the parody continues, but in a slighter form: he has "two horns like a lamb.") In the Beast they receive their detailed exposition. Let us begin with the heads. They are seven kings, of whom it appears that the Beast himself is one. This is to our minds extremely confusing, but according to St John's symbolical conventions it is perfectly correct. The astral woman of chapter 12 wears the twelve zodiacal signs as a crown on her head, and this means that she is one of those signs (Virgo), and, from the point of view there taken, the chief of them (the sign of priestly Levi, the jasper). So, of the seven kings, the Beast is one, and the chief.

The seven are given a form which makes them a perfect parody of the week of divine action, as it occurs over and over again in the Apocalypse. Five have had their day, the sixth reigns: there will be a seventh whose reign, like the sabbath, will be but an interlude ("He must remain a little while"). The great manifestation of power awaits the eighth; but the eighth day is not a new day, it is an eighth-and-first, and this expresses the fact that it is a day of resurrection, for one of the seven is reborn in it. So too the Beast is an eighth, but only in being one of the seven returned from the Abyss, a demonic resurrection in parody of the resurrection of Christ.

At this point the Genesis oracle on the Serpent and his seed comes to bear. "The woman's seed shall strike thy head, and thou shalt strike his heel." The serpent's seed par excellence, the Beast who is the eighth king, appears as the stricken head. The wound he bears is the stroke of the sword, the stroke of death; for it is written, "God shall bring down his sword, the holy, great and strong, upon the Dragon, the fleeing Serpent, the Dragon the crooked serpent, and the Dragon shall he slay" (Isa. 27:1). And yet, according to Genesis, it is *after* the serpent has been so smitten by God through the hand of the woman's seed, that he strikes the woman's seed in the heel. How can he, bearing already the stroke of the sword which is the stroke of death? Here is a mystery: the deadly stroke has been healed, but only for a time.

The Scriptures directly apply this mystery to the serpent, rather than to his seed. St John applies it to both. As to the serpent, he has been smitten through the merits of the Woman's Seed, and cast down from heaven to earth (as it is written, Upon thy belly shalt thou go, and earth shalt thou eat), before he ever turns to bite the heels of "the rest of the woman's seed." It is for the purpose of this heel-biting that he sets up the kingdom of the Beast; and the Beast is seen to be, like his master, one whom the sword of God has already smitten to death. The theme recurs in chapter 20. When the Dragon raises the rebellion of Gog and Magog against the saints, he appears as one escaped by divine permission from the Abyss, into which he had been cast after the Sword of the Word of God had struck him down in the great battle. The stroke of his death has been healed; but only for a moment, and he falls into a worse death, the lake of fire which burns with brimstone.

The theme, then, is applied to the Dragon, but with even greater emphasis to the Beast, and that for two reasons: because the Beast is the parody of Christ, so that the return of his stricken head from the Abyss becomes the parody of Christ's passion and resurrection; and because the Beast is a mortal man, so that the stroke of death means in his case something to which a precise sense can be attached. If a man has died, he has died, and if he reappears and acts on earth, it is certainly a wonder. But if we are told that a demon has been mortally stricken by the sword of God, and yet has reappeared to plague us, we do not see at once what is meant. Since he is not a bodily creature, his death-stroke cannot mean that he was sundered from the body that owned him before: and if it does not mean that, what can it mean but the annihilation of the spirit? But that it cannot mean, for the annihilated cannot return. In fact, the "deaths" of Satan are (a) his casting down from heaven, (b) his imprisonment in the Abyss: and these things befalling an incorporeal spirit do not have to our imaginations the force of death.

Christ, a Lamb standing as slaughtered, is the symbol of all saving power: Antichrist, a Beast slaughtered to the death and healed, is the quintessence of demonic unreality. How does St John conceive the nature of the difference between the two deaths? The key to it lies in the several qualities of death recognized by Jewish belief. The Old Testament for the most part regards death, and especially violent or premature death, as simply penal; the typical reward of virtue is length of days. This simple phase of belief belongs properly to the age before resurrection has been revealed. The Judaism of the first century believed passionately in resurrection. But the text of the Old Testament still stood: the doctrine of penal death could not be wholly evaded, but it could, and must, be qualified. There are several qualities of death. First, there are the exemplary sinners like Korah (Num. 16:29–35) struck down red-handed by divine justice, and dying "both to this world and to that which is to come." Second, there are sinners like Achan, who die a death of discipline, giving glory to the God of Israel (Josh. 7:19–26). They are happy in receiving their punishment here: they die to this world, but live to that which is to come. (The class, somewhat surprisingly, includes many of the impenitent dying under discipline. St Paul thinks it likely that the excommunicate sinner may suffer "the destruction of the flesh, that the Spirit may be saved in the day of Jesus Christ" [1 Cor. 5:5]; for we "being judged by the Lord, are chastened that we may not be damned with the world" [1 Cor. 11:32]). Third, there are premature deaths which are not visibly penal, but may be regarded as an atonement for sins—for who has not sinned?—and as a prevention of evils. Fourth, there are heroic and meritorious deaths, "hallowings of the Name," which atone for the sins of others, and obtain for the martyr peculiar rewards in the world to come. Such deaths are in no sense penal.

St John moved in this circle of ideas, as we can see from his adoption of the Rabbinic distinction between the first death (to this world) and the second (to the world to come). He even adds his own elaboration, a parallel doctrine of two resurrections. The first resurrection (to this world, in the millennium) is the privilege of martyrs, and also assures a part in the second resurrection (to the world to come, at the last day). The violent death of Antichrist, which terminated his first earthly reign, was like the death of Korah. He is a heathen man, and an enemy of God, and by his violent death he dies to this world, and to that which is to come. Thus, if he is allowed to return to earth, it is as a man already dead and damned, his name utterly expunged from the Book of Life. In relation to God's world, he is nothingness incarnate, he is already annihilated: and those who take part with him and take his name upon them take upon themselves an already achieved annihilation. Christ's death is of the opposite quality. It is wholly heroic, wholly meritorious, in dying it he has put death already behind his back, both the death to this world, and the death to that which is to come. Those who partake with him and take his Name upon them, take on themselves victorious and eternal life. Christ "lives, and became dead, and lives into ages unending": Antichrist "was, and is not, and will be here, and goes his way to perdition."

As the epitome of not-being, as the type of a working lie, he is the perfect object of idolatrous worship, for the idols, we know, are nothing in the world, and those that worship them are like unto them.

It remains to consider the historical application of St John's figure. We have hoped to show that all the features of it are significant, apart from any particular historical facts. St John has applied it to history: he did not shape it from history. The application may seem to us a trifle arbitrary, but that will not, in the circumstances, be surprising. The scheme of the seven heads is being fitted upon the Roman Emperors ready made, almost as it has been since by perverse expositors on an Antichrist at Rome or Paris or Berlin.

Irenaeus says that the Apocalypse was seen under Domitian, and almost any other date presents difficulties of an internal kind. So let Domitian be "the sixth who now is." If we consider the scheme of the week in general, we shall presume that the sixth represents a climax only second to the final climax in the eighth. Thus what St John will be saying to the Christians is this: "Things are as bad as they ever have been, but this is not the end. This monster will die, and be succeeded by a short-lived emperor. After him will come the Antichrist, and the appalling three-and-a-half years of unrestricted persecution. Then your deliverance will be."

If Domitian is the sixth, who are the previous five? It is impossible to be sure, because we do not know what to do with the three pretenders who succeeded Nero. If we count none of them, the five are Caius, Claudius, Nero, Vespasian and Titus, the "bestial" phase of the empire being dated from the beginning of open self-deification by an Emperor. If we count two of the three pretenders (a reasonable thing, perhaps, since Vitellius was never recognised by the ultimately victorious party), we shall have Nero, Galba, Otho, Vespasian and Titus, and we shall date "bestiality" from the beginning of organised persecution against the Church. No third solution appears to have much to be said for it. In any case the scheme of the week requires that the one of the seven who returns as an eighth should be in fact the first. Thus according to the one hypothesis the Antichrist will be Caligula *redivivus,* on the other he will be Nero *redivivus.*

Between these two suppositions there is little to choose. Both emperors received the death-wound. On the side of Caligula it may be said that he more exactly fits the type of Antichrist—that is to say, the type of Antiochus Epiphanes, both as himself and as projected back upon the person of Nebuchadnezzar by the author of Daniel. On the side of Nero it may be said, and has been said a great many times, that there was, anyhow, an expectation of his mysterious return; whereas no such expectation was ever held about Caius Caligula. It is also said that the 666 is to extracted from "Nero Caesar" in a Hebrew form. We have objected [elsewhere] to the last point as unnecessary: the 666 already has an embarrassing number of senses apart from it, and anyhow St John does his cryptograms in Greek, not Hebrew, even including his divinations from the ineffable Name. The argument from the expectation of Nero's return is somewhat impaired by the date at which we must suppose the Apocalypse to have been composed. The original form of Nero legend was simply that he had never died, but was in hiding with the Parthians: there actually appeared false Neros in the East. This form of the legend will do at a pinch, but it is not perfectly appropriate; for according to it Nero is not "dead and damned" when he returns. At a later date, when one had to admit that Nero must have died, a fantastic belief arose in Jewish (and Christian) circles, that he would return from the dead. This is the form of the legend which we really want; but it is difficult to suppose that it had got going before the beginning of the second century. In 95 (supposing that St John wrote about that year) Nero would not even have been an old man if he were alive, so why should the myth yet have abandoned its original and natural form, the restoration with Parthian aid of a Nero in hiding?

In view of these considerations, it may be wise to allow superior weight to the claims of Caligula. If it can be said that Nero made an impression on subsequent tradition in the role of Antichrist and *revenant,* it can be said with equal assurance that Caligula had left his mark on previous tradition; and it can be added with no hesitation at all that St John is more likely to have been influenced by his predecessors than by his successors. Caius Caligula, among his other foolish ideas, revived the exact project of Epiphanes, to bring the Jews to heel by erecting a heathen image bearing his own features in the City of Jerusalem. The scheme was never carried out, because the imperial official whose business it was prudently temporized, and meanwhile Caligula received the stroke of death, he was smitten by the Providence which had saved the Temple out of the hands of Sennacherib. But the event naturally revived the Epiphanes idea in the minds of Jews and Christians. St Paul, writing to the Thessalonians, tells them that the Lawless One has yet to be manifested, one who sets himself up against everything called divine or worshipful, so that he even seats himself as God in the Temple of God. At present, says the Apostle, he cannot appear because of a restraining force or person, presumably the more sober spirit which suppressed Caligula and still held sway in the person of the reigning monarch. But a time will come when the hindrance will be removed. And then, presumably, one will appear who will execute all that Caligula dreamed.

It is reasonable to recognize the influence of the Caligula episode in the verbal form of the Lord's Prophecy as it is reported for us in Mark 13. Since the Son of Man figure has the Antichrist expectation for its background in Daniel, it is natural that the Antichrist emblem should play some part in Christ's prediction of the Son of Man's advent; but the particularity of reference in Mark 13:14 suggests something more. "When ye shall see the abomination of desolation standing where he ought not—let the reader divine the sense!—then let those in Judea flee to the mountains." The Emperor, St Mark wishes surely to say, is going to try it again one day, and he will succeed—for a while.

The simplest view, therefore, to take of the historical prediction in the Apocalypse is that it is the continuation of the Christian tradition which we read in St Paul and St Mark. The advent of the Son of Man will be the termination of a reign of Antichrist of which Epiphanes was the type, and Caligula the threat. Caligula was struck down by the sword, but he will, as it were, return from the dead. His blasphemy was against God's "Name and Temple" in Jerusalem: now the visible Temple has disappeared, he will return to blaspheme the invisible, "God's Name and Tabernacle, even them that tabernacle in heaven," the spiritual temple which is the Church (Rev. 13:6).

Since the details of the figure of Antichrist are so evidently worked out on the plane of symbolism, it is almost useless to ask precisely what St John meant by the statement that Domitian's next successor but one would be Caligula back from the dead. According to St Mark, Herod said that Christ was the Baptist risen from death, even though the two preachers were close contemporaries. If we rationalize this, all it can mean is that the power and spirit of John had transferred themselves to Jesus, with force redoubled by John's martyrdom; but the rationalization does not do justice to the spirit of the text. The synoptic Gospels themselves teach that John Baptist was the returning Elijah. Elijah's having been exempted from physical death had something to do with the expectation of his return. And yet the Baptist did not fall ready-grown from the sky, he was begotten by natural generation. It is, in fact, impossible to say what visible token, if any, St John would expect the Antichrist to show of his being Caius Caligula *redivivus:* or even in what he conceived the identity between the one person and the other to consist.

The question how far St John is tied down to particular historical prediction, has often been debated. It seems proper to give an antithetical answer. On the one hand he writes out of scripture, theology, and spiritual principle: he is writing about the Antichrist, not about the tendencies of Roman Imperial history. On the other hand the few verses in chapter 17 concerned with the Seven Heads either mean nothing, or they mean quite precisely that the second successor of the reigning monarch will be the Antichrist. St John is not to know that Domitian (if he is writing under Domitian) is going to be cut off by violent death, perhaps in a matter of months, or that he will be succeeded by so very short-lived a ruler as Nerva. In the event, the historical prediction of Antichrist was disappointed with surprising swiftness by Trajan's accession.

We, presumably, are unlikely to feel that the particular prediction as such was part of divine revelation; Providence has not permitted it to become a clear part of the inspired text, and we might even wonder how firmly St John himself was attached to it. The Antichrist scheme is a mode of representation, an inspired way of reviewing the existence of the Church under imperial rule. St John himself could give his figures several applications. In John 4 the images of Revelation 17 return. The sinful woman seated on many waters becomes the Samaritaness by the well. It is the *sixth* hour. The Samaritan "harlot" has suffered under five "men" since she first, as Ezekiel says, wantoned with the Assyrian: Assyria, Babylon, Media, Persia and Greece have all possessed her. (The Median Empire did not include Palestine, but the Jews thought it had done so. This is plain in Daniel.) She disowns Caesar, the sixth who now is, and looks for the Messiah; already she accepts him in the Spirit, though his visible kingdom has not yet displaced that of Rome. (By contrast, her unhappy sister, Jerusalem, rejects Messiah at the same *sixth* hour, crying, "We have no king but Caesar"). Here the woman is still a city (not Babylon, but Samaria-Shechem). Her royal lover is still imperial tyranny, but the succession which brings us to "the sixth who now is" is a succession of empires, not of individual monarchs. The principle is still the same: we are in the end of the working week of political slavery. The final struggle and the victory of the Son of Man is upon us, whatever temporary disasters may preface it.

So much for the seven heads. There is less to be said about the ten horns. Various Scriptures suggest a league of kings against the Lord and his Israel at the last battle, Psalms 2 and 110, to search no further. The Daniel prophecies, on the other hand, give the Beast a monopoly of world power. St John reconciles the two pictures. The imperial power appears, in fact, to be absolute (there is, of course, Parthia, but that is only one king more). But in the last days ten kings who have as yet received no power will receive it, and make no use of it save to make common cause with the Beast in all things. If St John is thinking politically at all, he may be thinking of Antichrist as the orientalizing type of Emperor who substitutes subject kingdoms for provinces, so that he may rejoice in the title "King of Kings." And this agrees with the suggestions of the context: "They will war with the Lamb and he shall conquer them, for he is Lord of Lords and *King of Kings*."

If it is true for the most part that the Beast is written out of scripture and principle rather than out of contemporary history, the same is even more generally true of the False Prophet. It has often been suggested that he stands for the official priesthood of the Emperor-Cult, but the picture of such decorous and mundane dignitaries invoking fire from heaven or conjuring a voice out of a statue hardly fits. St John is thinking rather of the text of Deuteronomy, where we are warned that those who preach idolatry are not to be followed, whatever prophetical signs they may give. The False Prophet is to be set in contrasting parallel with the Two Witnesses, as the Beast is with the Lamb. St John himself is, indeed, a Christian Prophet, but the image-type of the function obtains free expression in the symbolical pair of martyrs. They also call down fire, not as a strengthless sign, but, like the fire of Elias, to devour their enemies. The False Prophet causes breath to enter the image of the Beast, that it may command those who refuse idolatry to be slain. When the true prophets have been slain for this very cause, and have lain three days and a half unburied, the Breath of God enters into them and raises them up.

Why, we may finally ask, does the divine Goodness permit the great rebellion of Antichrist? It is, we must answer, part of the economy of judgement. When Elijah on Mt Carmel said to the people, "How long halt ye between two opinions? If the Lord is God, serve him, if Baal, serve him," they answered never a word, for it seemed to them very natural that the God of Israel should be worshipped on his days at Bethel or Dan, and the Baal of Tyre on his days in Jezebel's embassy-chapel. Elijah forced a trial of strength with Baal, and the men of Israel were compelled to choose: divine mercy sealed the seven thousand who bowed not the knee to Baal, and divine vengeance cut off all whose lips had kissed him. The world commonly presents the outward appearance of so many million lives evading from the cradle to the grave every fundamental decision, and even the self-knowledge whether they are servants of God or of Mammon. The great drama of Christ and Antichrist forces the issue: there is no motive for refusing the mark of the Beast except that one bears the mark of Christ, nor any, heaven knows, for receiving the mark of Christ except that one loves him. The demons and their human instruments make saints of the believers, and heroes of the saints: and by their industrious scavenging they collect all the refuse of the world, and pile it conveniently for the fires of gehenna.

The saints are secure in their predestination. The demonic attack is directed against them, but it turns always upon the wicked. The Dragon attacks the woman crowned with stars: he cannot touch her, and the swinging of his tail brings down the apostate third, already ruled out of the heavenly temple by the word of God in the measuring vision. Defeated in the court of heaven, he falls to earth full of wrath. A heavenly voice declares that his descent is a matter of rejoicing for those who tabernacle in heaven, and of woe to men whose only home is earth. He pursues the heavenly woman into the wilderness, and shoots a river after her, which the earth-angel swallows, and the woman is saved. But when with his confederates Satan gathers the wicked Kings to Armageddon, the angel has been beforehand with him: he has dried the river to ease their passage, before the deceiving spirits have even started on their mission of persuading the kings to come. The Mother of Messiah is pursued by the "floods of Belial," but they do not come nigh her: the Great Harlot is peacably enthroned on the many waters, yet they rise against her. Evil turns always against evil.

The two constituent parts of pagan power are military kingship and urban wealth. Ever since the days of Alexander the two have been unhappily adjusted. The military emperor is a god and protector to the city, he woos and flatters her, she affects to worship him. But she hopes devoutly that he will keep his armies at a comfortable distance. From time to time, whether through lack of money or through the mutiny of his troops, or through his own cruelty or spite, he moves against the city and pillages her. Such are the loves and the quarrels of the Beast and Babylon, the parody of that marriage that there is betwixt Christ and his Church, the heavenly Jerusalem. Jerusalem is a city, yet she is also the garden of Paradise, fresh and clean. Cast forth from her gates, consigned to outer darkness and consuming fire, are all the filth and perversion of the life of cities.

Typology: Apocalypse

Northrop Frye

The Greek word for revelation, *apocalypsis,* has the metaphorical sense of uncovering or taking a lid off, and similarly the word for truth, *aletheia,* begins with a negative particle which suggests that truth was originally thought of as also a kind of unveiling, a removal of the curtains of forgetfulness in the mind. In more modern terms, perhaps what blocks truth and the emerging of revelation is not forgetting but repression. We have noted [elsewhere] that the last book in the Bible, the one explicitly called Revelation or Apocalypse, is a mosaic of allusions to the Old Testament: that is, it is a progression of antitypes. The author speaks of setting down what he has seen in a vision, but the Book of Revelation is not a visualized book in the ordinary sense of the word, as any illustrator who has struggled with its seven-headed and ten-horned monsters will testify. What the seer in Patmos had a vision of was primarily, as he conceived it, the true meaning of the Scriptures, and his dragons and horsemen and dissolving cosmos were what he saw in Ezekiel and Zechariah, whatever or however he saw on Patmos.

The general material of the vision is the familiar material of prophecy: there is again a *culbute générale* in which the people of God are raised into recognition and the heathen kingdoms are cast into darkness. There are portentous events in both social and natural orders: plagues, wars, famines, great stars falling from heaven, and an eventual transformation, for those who persist in the faith, of the world into a new heaven and earth. We are greatly oversimplifying the vision, however, if we think of

From *The Great Code: The Bible and Literature.* © 1981, 1982 by Northrop Frye. Harcourt Brace Jovanovich, 1982.

it simply as what the author thought was soon going to happen, as a firework show that would be put on for the benefit of the faithful, starting perhaps next Tuesday. For him all these incredible wonders are the inner meaning or, more accurately, the inner form of everything that is happening now. Man creates what he calls history as a screen to conceal the workings of the apocalypse from himself.

St. John the Divine sees all this "in the Spirit" (1:10), with his spiritual body, and the spiritual body is the most deeply repressed element of experience. The culbute he describes is political in only one of its aspects. The chief enemy, symbolized as a "Great Whore," is "spiritually" called Babylon, but she is also called "Mystery" (17:5). The word "mystery" is extensively used in the New Testament in both a good and a bad sense: there is a mystery of the kingdom (Matt. 13:11 and elsewhere) and a mystery of iniquity (2 Thess. 2:7). Nothing is more mysterious to the world than the half-esoteric beliefs of the primitive Christians, and nothing more obvious and apparent than, say, the power of the Emperor Nero. But the mystery turns into a revelation of how things really are, and the obvious power of Nero rolls into the darkness of the mystery of the corrupted human will from whence it emerged. The vision of the apocalypse is the vision of the total meaning of the Scriptures, and may break on anyone at any time. It comes like a thief in the night (Rev. 16:15, cf. 1 Thess. 5:2: this phrase is one of the few links between Revelation and the rest of the New Testament). What is symbolized as the destruction of the order of nature is the destruction of the way of seeing that order that keeps man confined to the world of time and history as we know them. This destruction is what the Scripture is intended to achieve.

There are, then, two aspects of the apocalyptic vision. One is what we may call the panoramic apocalypse, the vision of staggering marvels placed in a near future and just before the end of time. As a panorama, we look at it passively, which means that it is objective to us. This in turn means that it is essentially a projection of the subjective "knowledge of good and evil" acquired at the fall. That knowledge, we now see, was wholly within the framework of law: it is contained by a final "judgment," where the world disappears into its two unending constituents, a heaven and a hell, into one of which man automatically goes, depending on the relative strength of the cases of the prosecution and the defense. Even in heaven, the legal vision tells us, he remains eternally a creature, praising his Creator unendingly.

Anyone coming "cold" to the Book of Revelation, without context of any kind, would probably regard it as simply an insane rhapsody. It has been described as a book that either finds a man mad or else leaves him so. And yet, if we were to explore below the repressions in our own minds that keep us "normal," we might find very similar nightmares of anxiety and triumph. As a parallel example, we may cite the so-called Tibetan Book of the Dead, where the soul is assumed immediately after death to be going through a series of visions, first of peaceful and then of wrathful deities. A priest reads the book into the ear of the corpse, who is also assumed to hear the reader's voice telling him that all these visions are simply his own repressed mental forms now released by death and coming to the surface. If he could realize that, he would immediately be delivered from their power, because it is his own power.

If we take a similar approach to the Book of Revelation, we find, I think, that there is a second or participating apocalypse following the panoramic one. The panoramic apocalypse ends with the restoration of the tree and water of life, the two elements of the original creation. But perhaps, like other restorations, this one is a type of something else, a resurrection or upward metamorphosis to a new beginning that is now present. We notice that while the Book of Revelation seems to be emphatically the end of the Bible, it is a remarkably open end. It contains such statements as "Behold, I make all things new" (21:5); it describes God as the Alpha and Omega, the beginning and end of all possibilities of verbal expression; it follows the vision of the restoring of the water of life with an earnest invitation to drink of it. The panoramic apocalypse gives way, at the end, to a second apocalypse that, ideally, begins in the reader's mind as soon as he has finished reading, a vision that passes through the legalized vision of ordeals and trials and judgments and comes out into a second life. In this second life the creator-creature, divine-human antithetical tension has ceased to exist, and the sense of the transcendent person and the split of subject and object no longer limit our vision. After the "last judgment," the law loses its last hold on us, which is the hold of the legal vision that ends there.

We suggested [elsewhere] that the Bible deliberately blocks off the sense of the referential from itself: it is not a book pointing to a historical presence outside it, but a book that identifies itself with that presence. At the end the reader, also, is invited to identify himself with the book. Milton suggests that the ultimate authority in the Christian religion is what he calls the Word of God in the heart, which is superior even to the Bible itself, because for Milton this "heart" belongs not to the subjective reader but to the Holy Spirit. That is, the reader completes the visionary operation of the Bible by throwing out the subjective fallacy along with the objective one. The apocalypse is the way the world looks after the ego has disappeared.

In our discussion of creation we were puzzled by the paradox in the word when applied to human activity. God, we are told, made a "good" world; man fell into a bad world and the good one vanished; consequently *human* creativity has in it the quality of *re*-creation, of salvaging something with a human meaning out of the alienation of nature. At the end of the Book of Revelation, with such phrases as "I make all things new" (21:5) and the promise of a new heaven and earth, we reach the antitype of all antitypes, the real beginning of light and sound of which the first word of the Bible is the type.

The Power of Apocalyptic Rhetoric—Catharsis

Adela Yarbro Collins

The purpose of this [essay] is to show *what* the Book of Revelation does and *how* it does it. In other words, this [essay] focuses on the effect the Apocalypse had on its first readers and how it achieved that effect. The task of Revelation was to overcome the unbearable tension perceived by the author between what was and what ought to have been. His purpose was to create that tension for readers unaware of it, to heighten it for those who felt it already, and then to overcome it in an act of literary imagination. In the literary creation which is the Apocalypse, the tension between what was and what ought to be is manifest in the opposition between symbols of God's rule and symbols of Satan's rule, between symbols of the authority and power of Christ and symbols of the authority and power of Caesar.

When one reflects upon the symbols of the Apocalypse in the light of its historical situation, one sees that its task is to overcome the intolerable tension between reality and hopeful faith. Sociologists speak of such tension as cognitive dissonance, a state of mind that arises when there is great disparity between expectations and reality. Tension between what is and what ought to be is reflected in Revelation in the sharp contradiction set up between symbols and sets of symbols. All living beings are given a place in a dualistic structure. At the pinnacle of power on one side is God, the Pantocrator, ruler of all (1:8). On the other is Satan, the Dragon, who has power, a throne, and great authority (13:2). Allied with God is the Lamb who was slain (5:6); this is the one like a

From *Crisis and Catharsis: The Power of Apocalypse.* © 1984 by Adela Yarbro Collins. Westminster Press, 1984.

son of man who died and is alive forevermore (1:18). Allied with Satan is the beast from the sea (13:1–2), which was wounded with a mortal wound and yet lived (13:3, 14). All the people of the earth are divided into two groups; those who have the seal of God on their foreheads and whose names are in the book of life (3:5, 12; 7:3; 20:4; 21:27; 22:4) and those who bear the mark of the beast and worship it (9:4; 13:8, 17; 14:9–11; 16:2; 20:15). There is also a sharp contrast drawn between the luxurious and voluptuous harlot, who represents Babylon, the earthly city of abominations (chap. 17) and the pure bride of the Lamb, who symbolizes Jerusalem, the heavenly city of salvation (19:7–8; 21:2, 9–11).

This literary tension reflects the political tension between the adherents of the kingdom of God and those of the kingdom of Caesar (11:15; 12:10; 16:10; 17:18). Both claim dominion over the whole earth and eternal rule. The sharp contradictions set up between symbols and sets of symbols suggest that the Apocalypse is mythic narrative as it is defined by the French anthropologist Claude Lévi-Strauss. He has argued that "the purpose of myth is to provide a logical model capable of overcoming a contradiction" (*Structural Anthropology*). Myths mediate unwelcome contradictions, that is, they make them appear less final and thus more acceptable. If the contradiction is real, mediation thus produces a theoretically infinite number of attempts at overcoming the contradiction, each different in detail, but the same in underlying structure. The impossibility, at least in John's circumstances and from his point of view, of mediating the contradiction between the rule of God and the rule of Caesar would help explain why we have so much repetition in the Apocalypse. Beginning with the seven seals, each series of seven is an attempt to overcome this contradiction. Each series is distinctive in its particular formulations of character and plot. Beneath this variety of surface texture, however, is the same formal structure. In each series the contradiction between followers of the Lamb and followers of the beast is presented and overcome by the triumph of the Lamb.

What Ought to Be

A vision of what ought to be is expressed in the symbols related to God and Christ in the Apocalypse. In chapter 4 God is portrayed as king and creator. God is the enthroned one surrounded by various officers of the heavenly court. The hymn of the elders acclaims God worthy of glory, honor, and power, because the enthroned one has created all things. Near the beginning of the book, God is given the title Pantocrator, ruler of all

(1:8). It is a common title of God in Revelation, occurring in eight other passages. One of the climaxes of the book is the announcement that "the kingdom of the world has become the kingdom of our Lord and of his Christ, and he shall reign for ever and ever" (11:15).

In chapter 1, verse 5, Jesus is called the ruler of the kings of the earth. In the message to Pergamum, the sharp two-edged sword of the one like a son of man is implicitly contrasted with the "sword" of the Roman governor which slew Antipas (2:12–13). The son of God is portrayed as the one who has power over the nations (2:18, 26–27). The exalted Christ is enthroned with God (3:21). He is given the traditional national messianic titles "Lion of the tribe of Judah" and "the Root of David" (5:5). He is given the titles "King of kings" and "Lord of lords," which have obvious political connotations (19:16). He is portrayed as king in the messianic reign of a thousand years (20:4–6).

These symbols and their use in Revelation suggest that some early Christians expected the rule of God announced by Jesus to be a public affair. They expected God's rule to involve the whole person, the outer as well as the inner self. They expected the social, economic, and political order to be changed, speedily and thoroughly, not just that another voluntary association would take its place beside the others. This public transformation of reality was expected to involve at least autonomy for the faithful, if not power over others. All the faithful have been made priests (1:6; 5:10). The one who conquers will rule over the nations with a rod of iron (2:27). All the faithful will reign on earth (5:10; see also 22:5).

The early Christian perspective reflected in the Apocalypse shares with the Zealots and related Jewish groups the conviction that God's rule must be manifest in concrete political ways and that acknowledgment of God's rule is incompatible with submission to Rome. "Behold, he is coming with the clouds, and every eye will see him, every one who pierced him; and all the tribes of the earth will wail on account of him. Even so. Amen" (1:7). The starting point of Revelation is that Jesus and his followers must have public and communal vindication, in the here and now and soon. The transformation of individuals, inner freedom, a personal afterlife—these elements alone were an insufficient, incomplete manifestation of salvation.

Such were the hopes, the expectations of what ought to be. In striking contrast to the hope was the reality. By the light of the historical context, we may read in the pages of Revelation evidence of a perceived social crisis and personal and communal trauma, as we saw [elsewhere].

The perceived social crisis and traumatic experiences apparently led to certain feelings that are reflected and dealt with in the Apocalypse. A feeling of powerlessness was evoked by the exclusion of Christians from Jewish and Gentile institutions. Fear was elicited by the denunciation of Christians before Roman authorities and by the impressions left by the traumas of Nero's persecution, the destruction of Jerusalem, the execution of Antipas, and John's banishment. Aggressive feelings were aroused by the various social tensions. Resentment was felt at the rejection and hostility of Jews and Gentiles. Envy of the autonomous, the wealthy, and the powerful rankled. The imperial ruler cult evoked antipathy and frustration. The violent deeds of the Roman Empire called forth a desire for vengeance.

How the Apocalypse Creates Its Effect

In reflecting upon how the Apocalypse does what it does, the first thing to consider is the type of language to which it belongs. Words are used in a wide variety of ways, among which are (1) to talk about people, things, and ideas (informative language); (2) to think (cognitive language); (3) to display attitudes and feelings (expressive language); (4) to elicit attitudes and feelings (evocative language). Informative and cognitive language may be called referential, in that the words refer to generally recognizable entities.

To some extent the language of the Book of Revelation is referential. It is that quality which allows us to relate the book to its historical context and to discover social information in its pages. But the primary purpose of the book is not to impart information. It is rather to call for *commitment* to the actions, attitudes, and feelings uttered. It is thus primarily commissive language. In particular, it is expressive and evocative language. It makes no attempt to report events or to describe people in a way that everyone could accept. Rather, it provides a highly selective and perspectival view. Like a poem, it presents and interprets some aspect of reality, expresses a response to it, and invites the reader or hearer to share in the interpretation and the response.

As expressive language, the book of Revelation creates a virtual experience for the hearer or reader. It is likely that the Apocalypse was read aloud before the assembled Christians of a given locality, perhaps at regular intervals. A beatitude is pronounced near the beginning, "Blessed is he who reads aloud the words of the prophecy, and blessed are those who hear, and who keep what is written therein; for the time is near"

(1:3). For this reason it is better to speak of the first "hearers" of Revelation, rather than the "readers."

The Apocalypse is as evocative as it is expressive. Not only does it display attitudes and feelings; it also elicits them. One can go even further and say that the Apocalypse creates its effect by manipulating the thoughts, attitudes, and feelings of the hearers. I am using the word "manipulate" here in the neutral sense of handling with skill or art. I do not intend the negative sense of unfairness, fraud, or falsification due to self-interest. The Apocalypse handles skillfully the hearers' thoughts, attitudes, and feelings by the use of effective symbols and a narrative plot that invites imaginative participation. This combination of effective symbols and artful plot is the key to the power of apocalyptic rhetoric.

NARRATIVE TECHNIQUES AND THEIR EMOTIONAL EFFECT

Various techniques may be observed in the use of effective symbols and the construction of plot. The most fundamental technique and the one that underlies and reinforces all the others is the presentation of the Apocalypse as an authoritative, true, and trustworthy revelation of heavenly origin. It is claimed that the revelation comes from the highest authority, from God, who gave it to Jesus Christ, who entrusted it to an angel, who communicated it to John (1:1). The hearer is assured of the truthfulness of John's testimony (1:2). This characterization of the content of the book is reinforced by the use of vision accounts and the reports of auditions. The hearer is given the impression that John is handing on the revelation just as he received it. The claims and assurances about the origin and reliability of the revelation are repeated several times near the end of the book (22:6–10, 16; see also 18–20). It is likely that the effectiveness of the Apocalypse for the first hearers depended upon belief in these claims. Such belief is very important today for fundamentalist readers of Revelation. Critical readers, however, take the position that the validity of the book must be determined through an assessment of its content, quite apart from the question of its origin.

A second technique is the reinterpretation of prophecy and of other texts in the Jewish Bible read as prophecy. The effectiveness of this technique depended on the continuing belief in the authority and reliability of the prophets of the Jewish Bible and on the assumption that they prophesied, not about their own times, but about the end of days. Like the Essenes at Qumran, the early Christians believed that they were living during the last days. As the Essenes believed that their Teacher of

Righteousness had received the interpretative key by divine revelation to the mysteries of the biblical texts, so the early Christians believed that their prophets, apostles, and teachers could expound the true meaning of such texts, because they were enlightened by the teaching of Jesus Christ and the Holy Spirit.

This technique is evident in a saying quoted earlier [in *Crisis and Catharsis*], "Behold, he is coming with the clouds, and every eye will see him, every one who pierced him; and all the tribes of the earth will wail on account of him" (1:7). The mysterious description of one like a son of man in Daniel 7:13 and the obscure prediction of Zechariah 12:10–14 are regarded as unfulfilled prophecies. The two are combined and reinterpreted as a prediction of the second coming of Christ as judge in the Final Judgment. The underlying conviction is that Daniel and Zechariah predicted events in the near future of the hearers of Revelation.

Just as the book of Daniel updated and reinterpreted Jeremiah's prophecy that the desolations of Jerusalem would last seventy years, so the book of Revelation reinterprets and applies to its own situation the prophecy in Daniel that the shattering of the power of the holy people would last for a time, two times, and half a time (Dan. 7:25; 12:7). Each "time" in Daniel represents about a year (see Dan. 8:13–14; 9:27; 12:11–12). The vision of the angel who announces the nearness of the end in Revelation 10 is heavily reminiscent of the angel in Daniel 12 who says that salvation will come after three and a half "times." The Gentiles, it is predicted, will trample the holy city for forty-two months (three and one half years; Rev. 11:2). The two witnesses will prophesy for one thousand two hundred and sixty days (three and one half years; 11:3). The woman clothed with the sun, it is said, will be nourished in the desert for a time, and times, and a half a time (12:14). Earlier her sojourn is described as lasting one thousand two hundred and sixty days (three and a half years, 12:6). Finally, the beast from the sea will exercise authority for forty-two months (three and a half years; 13:5). It is quite easy to conclude that the author of Daniel actually made calculations and to associate the three and one half years with the period between the defilement of the temple and its rededication. It is virtually impossible to do anything of the sort with Revelation. It is likely that John adopted the designation of a period of final crisis from Daniel and believed that the prophecy of Daniel 12 would be fulfilled in his own time. It is unlikely that he made any precise calculations.

When Daniel 7 was composed, the fourth and most terrifying beast represented the Greco-Syrian kingdom with which its first readers had to contend. In chapter 13, the fourth beast of Daniel (or perhaps all four beasts combined) is interpreted as a prophecy of the Roman Empire. If John knew of the application of Daniel 7 to the situation under Antiochus Epiphanes, he would have considered it incorrect or merely preliminary. Daniel was viewed as a prophecy referring to John's and his hearers' own time.

Another literary technique is the use of traditional symbols in the composition of allegorical narrative. A borderline case between this technique and the previous one is the use of the names Balaam and Jezebel in the messages to Pergamum and Thyatira. From one point of view, the hearers could infer that the narratives in Numbers and 1 and 2 Kings were written for the instruction of the believers of the last days and that the characters Balaam and Jezebel in those narratives were really false teachers contemporary with themselves. From another point of view, these names were already traditional symbols. The hearers were being invited to see analogies between classic situations in Israel's past and their own situations. They were being called upon to think typologically. Typology is a way of thinking that is similar to allegory. An archetype is used to give meaning to a present event. The effectiveness of this technique, if it be accepted, is obvious and powerful. The nameless man who had a following at Pergamum is no longer a fellow Christian who holds opinions and teaches practices that must be evaluated on their merits. Suddenly he is Balaam, who led Israel into idolatry and harlotry; these deeds angered the Lord and provoked him to send a plague upon Israel (Num. 25:1–9; 31:16). The implication for the hearers is plain: if they listen to this man's teaching they will be punished by God. The same dynamic is present in giving the name "Jezebel" to the prophet who had a following in Thyatira.

The allegorical technique is also evident in the visions of the seven trumpets and the seven bowls. Both the image of the trumpet and that of the bowl have their own connotations, which contribute to the effect of the narrative. The focus here is on the similarity these visions have with the narratives about the plagues against Egypt which the Lord sent through Moses, according to Exodus 7–12. Among the allusions are water turning to blood (Rev. 8:9; 16:4; Exod. 7:14–24) and a plague of locusts (Rev. 9:1–11; Exod. 10:1–20). The plagues of the trumpets and bowls are presented in Revelation as punishment upon the earth, especially upon the Romans, for the unjust shedding of blood, especially for the murder of faithful Christians. The use of the traditional symbol of the plague suggested to the hearers that they understand their own situation by analogy with the slavery of the Israelites in Egypt. The cognitive dissonance or tension between their expectations and their experience was reduced by suggesting that their own hardships would be resolved as those of the Israelite slaves were. As God delivered Israel from Egypt, so he would deliver Christians from Rome.

Perhaps the most powerful use of this technique is the presentation of the hearers' opponents as symbols of chaos and the resolution of the conflict between the hearers and their opponents through narratives whose plots conform to the traditional myths of combat and creation. Chapter 13 contains a vision of a beast rising out of the sea. Several elements suggest that this beast symbolizes the Roman Empire. It has dominion over the whole earth (v. 7b), it is worshiped by many people (vv. 4, 8), and it attacks the saints (v. 7a). The portrait of the beast from the sea draws upon a number of closely related traditional symbols. It contains allusions to features of Daniel 7 and 8. As we have seen, Daniel's vision of four kingdoms is presented indirectly as a prophecy fulfilled in Revelation's own time. But the images of Daniel were already traditional. The beasts rising from the sea called to mind Yahweh's battles with Leviathan and Rahab, those sea monsters whose rebellion against God symbolized the forces of chaos, sterility, and death. Their defeat represents the victory of order, fertility, and life, which is associated with God's creative acts. These symbols were not unique to Israel. They were common in narratives of combat and creation in various cultures of the ancient and the Hellenistic Near East. There are clear indications in Revelation that such symbols are not archaic survivals, but living symbols arising out of a mythopoetic consciousness.

The plots of ancient myths of combat vary, but they have certain elements in common. A rebellion, usually led by a dragon or other beast, threatens the reigning gods, or the king of the gods. Sometimes the ruling god is defeated, even killed, and then the dragon reigns in chaos for a time. Finally the beast is defeated by the god who ruled before, or some ally of his. Following his victory the reestablished king of the gods (or a new, young king in his stead) builds his house or temple, marries and produces offspring, or hosts a great banquet. These latter elements represent the reestablishment of order and fertility.

This basic plot or pattern is found in every series of visions in Revelation, beginning with the seven seals. It is found in brief form, for example, in chapter 12, and in more elaborate form, for example, in the passage that extends from 19:11 to 22:5. In chapter 12, the dragon rebels against God by attempting to destroy the agent of God who is about to be born. This hostile act implies that the dragon is attempting to become king himself. His association with chaos is clear from his sweeping down stars from the sky with his tail (v. 4). The battle comes in verses 7–9. Michael, ally of God and the child, defeats the dragon and casts him out of heaven. The result is the reestablishment of God's kingship in heaven (v. 10). But a further consequence of the casting down of the dragon is a dragon's reign on earth (vv. 12b–17). This reign is characterized by chaos, as the spewing out of water from the dragon's mouth shows.

In this chapter, verses 1–9 and 13–17 are narrative. Verses 10–12 comprise a hymn that provides a kind of commentary on the narrative. The dragon's attack on the woman and the child is interpreted as Satan's attempt to malign Christians in the heavenly court in his role as accuser. The throwing of the dragon down out of heaven is presented as equivalent to the victory of Christians over Satan by means of Christ's death, their own testimony, and their willingness to die. The image of the heavenly court calls earthly courts to mind. Although Christians who hold on to their faith are found guilty in the earthly courts, they are acquitted in the heavenly court, whose judgment alone truly matters. Thus, the hymn suggests that the narrative of chapter 12 is allegorical, not in the sense that each character or event in the story can be identified with some character or event in ordinary time, space, and history. Rather, it is allegorical in the sense that the whole narrative expresses in symbolic form the predicament of the hearers and provides it with a resolution. The hearers are invited to identify with the woman. Like Israel at the time of the Exodus she is carried to safety by eagles' wings. Like Israel she is nourished in the desert by God. The traditional narrative of the Exodus reinforces the narrative of chapter 12 in assuring the hearers that they will not be overwhelmed by the threat that Rome poses to them.

The passage that extends from 19:11 to 22:5 is the climax of the Apocalypse. As we have seen, the Book of Revelation consists of six sections apart from prologue and epilogue: (1) the seven messages, (2) the seven seals, (3) the seven trumpets, (4) seven unnumbered visions, (5) the seven bowls plus a Babylon appendix, (6) seven unnumbered visions plus a Jerusalem appendix. The seven messages constitute a distinct section in which the hearers are directly admonished and encouraged. The other five sections recapitulate each other; that is, they all have the same basic plot. As we have seen, each section implies a movement from persecution of the faithful, to punishment of the opponents of the faithful, to salvation of the faithful. This narrative movement which is repeated conforms to the basic plot shared by the ancient myths of combat: threat of rebellion, combat-victory (defeat of rebels), and kingship (salvation, order, fertility).

The last section of the Apocalypse begins with a theophany of the divine warrior (19:11–16). The threat or rebellion is presupposed. Verse 11 picks up a thread of narrative dropped at 16:16 where the dragon and the two beasts of chapter 13 are gathering the kings of the earth for the final battle. In 19:17–18 the victory banquet is depicted as a feast of birds upon the flesh of the fallen. In Isaiah 34:7 the bodies of the slain are portrayed as a sacrifice that makes the land fertile. The banquet motif in Revelation 19 reflects an ancient form of the idea that the hero's victory leads to renewed fertility. In the messianic reign (20:4–6) the kingdom of the newly established king, Christ, is manifested. The fertility of the restored order is expressed in the creation of a new heaven and earth (21:1) and in the manifestation of the water of life and the tree of life (22:1–2). Fertility and order are also expressed, at least in a sublimated way, in the sacred marriage of the Lamb (21:2, 9). The presentation of the new Jerusalem takes the place of temple-building or palace-building in other narratives.

The presentation of the hearers' struggle with Rome as a new form of the old conflict between order and chaos clarified their situation for the hearers and gave it meaning. The movement of the plot then instilled the conviction that the heavens ultimately would be victorious, as the forces of order always triumph in the myth. To be effective this narrative resolution of the crisis must be believable. The first hearers were likely to have found it so, since they were attuned to the perspective of myth, and since every people of the Greco-Roman world had at least one version of the combat or creation myth. The archaic and universal nature of the mythic pattern reflected in Revelation lends a certain authority and credence to its underlying message. As it was in the beginning, as it always has been when the chaos monster rears its head, so it will be once again. God and the Lamb, as representatives of creation, life, and order, will be victorious over the dragon and his two bestial allies.

It is likely that Revelation 11:3–13, the narrative about the two witnesses, has a function similar to that of the narrative about the woman and the dragon in chapter 12. The witnesses are identified as "the two olive trees and the two lampstands which stand before the Lord of the earth" (11:4). This identification calls to mind one of the visions of Zechariah. The prophet sees "two branches of the olive trees" and "two golden pipes from which the oil is poured out" (Zech. 4:12). An angel tells him that these represent "the two anointed who stand by the Lord of the whole earth" (Zech. 4:14). Once again, John is using an old story, traditional images, to interpret his own situation. In the context of Zechariah, the two anointed ones are the new Davidic ruler (Zerubbabel) and the new high priest (Joshua).

If John adverted to that interpretation at all, he would have seen Zerubbabel and Joshua as, at most, prototypes of the two witnesses of the end time. There is nothing in the Apocalypse that implies the coming of a Davidic and a priestly messiah. John's assumption probably was that the passage in Zechariah was about to be fulfilled in a way the Jewish prophet did not foresee. The activity of each of the witnesses recalls the mighty deeds of Moses and Elijah, as well as the ministry and destiny of Jesus. If "any one would harm them," they have power to destroy "their foes by fire." This element recalls one of the stories about Elijah (2 Kings 1:9–12; Sir. 48:3). Their "power to shut the sky, that no rain may fall during the days of their prophesying" recalls an even more famous story about Elijah (1 Kings 17–18; Sir. 48:3; Luke 4:25; James 5:17). The "power over the waters to turn them into blood, and to smite the earth with every plague" recalls the role of Moses as God's agent in smiting the Egyptians, especially his turning the Nile and all the waters of Egypt into blood (Exod. 7:14–19).

The two witnesses will be killed in Jerusalem, where "their Lord was crucified." Their bodies will lie unburied for "three days and a half"; then God will bring them back to life (v. 11). Finally, they will go up to heaven in a cloud (v. 12). The basic pattern of the witnesses' destiny very clearly repeats that of Jesus' ministry: a prophetic ministry including mighty deeds, violent death in Jerusalem, resurrection and ascension. The ascension of the two witnesses also reminds the hearers of Elijah's ascension in a chariot (2 Kings 2:11). Moses was also thought to have ascended to heaven. Such a tradition is probably reflected in Jude 9.

Many theories have been proposed on the identity of the two witnesses and the time of their appearance. One theory is that they are historical figures, Peter and Paul. Another theory holds that the vision is, from John's point of view, an as yet unfulfilled prophecy of the return of Moses and Elijah or of two superhuman forerunners of the second coming of Christ. It is difficult, if not impossible, to determine how John himself understood this vision. It is perhaps significant that he did not name the two witnesses. The anonymity of the witnesses suggests that the importance of the story was not so much its who or when, but the fact that it provides a point of orientation for the hearers. Like the two characters in the story, the hearers aspired to being God's witnesses, to giving testimony about God's cause in the world. At least it is clear that John wished them so to aspire. They too are confident of God's protection, even though they may be called upon to endure hardships, suffering, even violent death. God's protection is expected in their everyday lives and beyond and in spite of death. This protection is described in spectacular ways in the story. It may well be that John and the hearers of the book experienced and expected spectacular assistance. The ministry of Jesus, and that of at least some apostles and prophets, seems to have been accompanied by extraordinary phenomena such as healing and exorcism. The allusions to the signs of Elijah and Moses may be hyperbolic reflections of such phenomena, actual and expected. The hope of resurrection was probably held quite literally. It is striking that the witnesses are raised and ascend in the sight of their foes (vv. 11–12). That element reflects the desire for public vindication evident also in chapter 1, verse 7 and chapter 3 verse 9. In any case, the spectacular divine intervention expresses in a symbolic way the deep trust that God's cause, as John sees it, is just, true, and worth dying for. The intervention of God does not eliminate the necessity of dying.

Death in this narrative is at the hands of "the beast which ascends from the bottomless pit." The pit represents the underworld where the forces of chaos are often confined in the combat and creation myths. The ascension of the beast from the pit implies that the forces which oppose the testimony of God's witnesses are part of the constant struggle of death with life, of destruction with creation, of order with chaos.

The techniques just described are ways in which the thoughts, attitudes, and feelings of the hearers were skillfully handled. The feeling of powerlessness due to the marginal social situation of the hearers was mitigated by the assurance that they had access to privileged information, to revealed truth of heavenly origin. At a deeper level, the hearers' powerlessness and lack of control over events is not denied, but affirmed. It is of little importance, however, because they are God's and God is in control. The reinterpretation of prophecy and the use of typology and allegory imply that the course of events has been fixed. The forces of chaos are dominant now, but their defeat is certain.

Likewise, the fear of the hearers is not denied or minimized. On the contrary, it is intensified. The hostile Jews and Roman authorities are not just ill-disposed human beings, but they have all the power of Satan on their side. Just as death, disease, and the failure of crops are ever-recurring evils, so these hostile political forces will not be overcome easily. The symbols and plot promise victory and new life, but it is on the other side of suffering and death.

THE PROCESS OF CATHARSIS

There is a certain analogy between Aristotle's explanation of the function of Greek tragedy and the function of Revelation. In each case certain emotions are aroused and then a catharsis of those emotions is achieved. Tragedy manipulates the emotions of fear and pity; Revelation, primarily fear and resentment. Aristotle's term "catharsis" is a medical metaphor. In its medical sense it refers to the removal from the body of alien matter that is painful and the restoration of the system to its normal state. The relation between this medical sense and Aristotle's application of the term to tragedy has been much debated. He does not appear to have meant that the emotions of fear and pity are removed by tragedy, but only that their painful or disquieting elements are removed. Fear and pity in daily life can be disquieting for at least two reasons. Such feelings are often inarticulate, vague, and thus difficult to deal with. Also, they relate to people and events that are very close to home and thus especially threatening. This threatening character applies also to pity in Aristotle's understanding: we pity others where under like circumstances we would fear for ourselves. The emotions of the audience are purged in the sense that their feelings of fear and pity are intensified and given objective expression. The feelings are thus brought to consciousness and become less threatening.

Revelation functions in a similar way. Fear of Roman power is evoked or intensified. In various symbolic narratives, conflicts are described, each of which is a paradigm of the hearers' situation. As we have seen, the hearers' destiny is symbolized by the story of the two witnesses in chapter 11 and of the woman in chapter 12. The powers that threaten them are symbolized by the beast from the abyss and the dragon. These vivid images are certainly designed more to evoke terror than to allay it. Nevertheless, the projection of the conflict onto a cosmic screen, as it were, is cathartic in the sense that it clarifies and objectifies the conflict. Fearful feelings are vented by the very act of expressing them, especially in this larger-than-life and exaggerated way.

Resentment of Roman wealth and power is evoked or intensified especially in chapters 17 and 18. The great harlot Babylon is arrayed in purple and scarlet, adorned with gold, jewels, and pearls; she drinks from a golden cup (17:4; 18:16). The merchants are portrayed mourning over their cargo of luxury goods: "gold, silver, jewels and pearls, fine linen, purple, silk, and scarlet, all kinds of scented wood, all articles of ivory, all articles of costly wood, bronze, iron and marble, cinnamon, spice, incense, myrrh, frankincense, wine, oil, fine flour and wheat, cattle and sheep, horses and chariots, and slaves, that is, human souls" (18:12–13). This list is purposely selective and perspectival. The major cargo carried on Roman seas was grain. It was from the transportation of grain that the fortunes under the Flavians were made. This list emphasizes the luxury items, goods which the hearers either had no hope of attaining or were expected to forego. All these alluring, unattainable goods are to be destroyed by divine wrath.

Revelation produces a catharsis not only by means of individual symbolic narratives but by the structure of the book as a whole. Feelings of fear and resentment are released by the book's repeated presentations of the destruction of the hearers' enemies. The element of persecution represents the present, conflict-ridden, and threatened situation in which the author invites the hearers to see themselves. The second two elements in the repeated plot, judgment and salvation, represent the resolution of that situation: the persecutors are destroyed by divine wrath and the persecuted are exalted to a new, glorious mode of existence.

Psychological Dynamics

The effect of the symbols and plot of the Apocalypse was to reduce cognitive dissonance in two related ways. First, disquieting, disruptive feelings were released in a literary, experiential process of catharsis. Second, the conviction was instilled in the hearers that what ought to be *is*. The content of Revelation involves a hidden heavenly reality that shows the visible world to be radically different from what it seems. Jesus, though slain, is exalted in heaven and controls the destiny of the world (chap. 5). Although his followers are powerless, he is the true king, the ruler of the kings of the earth. In spite of the divine honors accorded to Rome and its agents, Satan is the real source of its power, not heaven (chaps. 12 and 13). What ought to be *is* also in the already determined future. The content of the book also involves a future reality in which the earthly realm will be fully and manifestly determined by the heavenly world, that is, by God and Christ. Although this process was probably not conscious, what ought to be was experienced as a present reality by the hearers in the linguistic and imaginative event of hearing the book read. If the book was read in the context of worship, this effect would have been even stronger. As a gathered community before God, the hearers would have experienced in the imagination the heavenly reality and the determined future in which John was calling them to believe.

From a social-psychological viewpoint, the vision of a heavenly reality and of a radically new future functions as compensation for the relatively disadvantaged situation of the hearers or as an imaginative way of resolving the tension between expectations and social reality. There is a certain analogy between the creative imagination of the schizophrenic and the vision of the Apocalypse. According to Harold Searles, the tragedy of a schizophrenic's life is very much of a piece with the tragedy of life for all human beings. Ernest Becker agreed and defined that tragedy as the fact of human finitude, one's dread of death, and the overwhelmingness of life. All human beings are faced with an existential dilemma. This dilemma is rooted, in Erich Fromm's words, in the fact that humankind is half animal and half symbolic. Our animal nature presents us with the necessity of living within certain limits. Our symbolic nature allows us to challenge those limits, to transcend them at least in the imagination, by the pursuit of possibility.

The schizophrenic feels the pain of the human existential dilemma more acutely than others because he or she does not have "the confident defenses that a person normally uses to deny" it. By means of elaborate fantasies, the schizophrenic is able to live with the terror of reality. In this mental state, a person overvalues the powers of the symbolic self and one loses oneself in the pursuit of possibility. Such a way of life is marvelously creative, but ultimately maladaptive and dysfunctional.

The Book of Revelation takes messianic language about Jesus very seriously and refuses to eliminate or minimize the social and political dimensions of messianic hope. As we have seen, such a preunderstanding made it very difficult if not impossible to make sense of the current sociopolitical situation of Christians. The solution of the Apocalypse is an act of creative imagination which, like that of the schizophrenic, withdraws from empirical reality, from real experience in the everyday world. According to the anthropologist George De Vos, an individual can deal with inner tensions by devising a projective system. It takes a great deal of energy to maintain such a system, however; if the burden of maintenance becomes unbearable, such an individual may lapse into pathological behavior. Inner stresses are more effectively controlled by collectively held and socially reinforced beliefs, since it takes less energy to believe in a social myth than to create and maintain one's own. De Vos goes on to say that social projections shared collectively within a group permit some form of psychic balance to be maintained without any overt social malfunctioning. Under ordinary conditions overt conflict does not appear. However, when stress becomes unmanageable, some overt form of violence may erupt.

("Conflict, Dominance, and Exploitation," in *Sanctions for Evil*)

These considerations call to mind two frequent criticisms of the Apocalypse. It is often said of the Book of Revelation and other apocalyptic texts that they are pessimistic, passive, a lapse from human activity into mythology. Similarly, millenarian movements have been called "prepolitical." These assessments are quite accurate to a point. It is God or some other superhuman figure who will act to bring in the millennium. Humanity is to endure and wait. As we have seen, John urged his readers indirectly to avoid participation in civic and political life. Nevertheless, the symbols and plot of Revelation, when deeply heard, do affect the actions of the hearers. It is a text that enables hearers or readers to cope in extreme circumstances. In a situation where direct political action is not feasible, it is a text that keeps alive the expectation of a better world.

Another criticism of the Apocalypse focuses on its violent language. It by no means advocates violence of humans against others. Nevertheless, violent imagery is prominent. The attitude toward violence in the book thus seems ambivalent. It can be explored in relation to the concept of aggression.

The Apocalypse may be viewed fruitfully as part of a process of containing aggressive feelings. As we have seen, it is likely that the social tensions evident in the historical setting of Revelation gave rise to aggressive feelings on the part of the author and some of the hearers. There was probably resentment at the rejection and hostility of many Jews and Gentiles, envy and resentment of the autonomous, wealthy, and powerful, a desire for vengeance against Rome, and competitive and even hostile feelings toward other Christians with whom one disagreed. The Book of Revelation provides evidence for a dynamic process involving two methods of containing such aggressive feelings.

The first of these is the transference of aggression felt by the author or the hearers to another subject. When aggressive action is not desirable and aggressive feelings cannot simply be suppressed or converted into other feelings and activities, the aggressive feelings may be transferred. Such transference relieves some of the tension related to the aggression and defuses the human relationships involved.

In the messages, John's apparent hostility to his opponents is transferred to the one like a son of man. Christ will make war with the sword of his mouth against the Pergamenes who follow "Balaam" and the Nicolaitans (2:16). The son of God will throw "Jezebel" into a sickbed and those who follow her he will throw into tribulation or strike dead (2:22–23).

In the fifth seal, the souls of the slain cry out for vengeance upon "those who dwell on earth" (6:10). This cry is a thin veil over the hearers' desire for vengeance on Rome. They do not fight Rome directly; rather, they pray to God to vindicate them. The aggression is transferred to God. In the sixth seal, the eschatological woes are described, including the rolling up of the sky like a scroll and the removal of islands and mountains. Naturally, all humanity is affected. Yet the depiction of distress focuses on the cries of the mighty, of kings, great men, generals, the rich and strong. The aggression of the powerless toward the powerful is expressed here. It is transferred to God and the Lamb. The last day is the day of *their* wrath.

In the second half of the book (chaps. 12–22), vengeance is wreaked particularly against Rome. When the seventh angel poured out his bowl, the great city split into three parts and "God remembered great Babylon, to make her drain the cup of the fury of his wrath" (16:19). A great multitude in heaven is heard saying, "Hallelujah! Salvation and glory and power belong to our God, for his judgments are true and just; he has judged the great harlot who corrupted the earth with her fornication, and he has avenged on her the blood of his servants" (19:1–2). The hearers' hostility to Rome is transferred to another subject, namely, God.

In each of the cases in which aggression is transferred to another subject, it is also transposed from the present to the future. John the prophet was in conflict with "Balaam," with the Nicolaitans, and with "Jezebel" at the time Revelation was written. The aggressive feelings he probably felt were a matter of the present from his point of view. The resolution of the conflict, however, is presented indirectly as belonging to the future. The Christ of the message to the Pergamenes says, "I *will come* to you *soon* and war against them ["Balaam" and the Nicolaitans] with the sword of my mouth" (2:16; emphasis added). With regard to "Jezebel" and her followers, the threatened judgment by Christ is also future (2:22–23). The eschatological woes (6:12–17) and the destruction of "Babylon" (16:19) are events expected by John and the hearers in the near future. The announcements of these events are in the past tense only because they report John's visions. The visions took place in the past, but the events they foreshadow are yet to come. This transposition of aggressive feelings into imagined aggressive acts in the future is another way of alleviating the tension awakened by such feelings.

The second method of containing aggression reflected in Revelation is that of internalizing it and reversing it, so that it falls on the subject of the aggressive feelings. This process may explain the intensification of norms which the Apocalypse expresses and evokes. If John and some of the hearers turned their aggression inward, this would explain why they became more demanding of themselves and other Christians with regard to assimilation, wealth, sexuality, and the urge toward self-preservation.

The messages to Ephesus, Pergamum, and Thyatira oppose tendencies to assimilation on the part of some Christians. They thus intensify the early Christian norm of exclusivism with regard to Greco-Roman culture, especially its polytheistic aspect. The origin of this intensified norm in aggressive feeling is evident in the highly negative language used to describe the opponents themselves, with their teachings and practices, and in the violently threatening language used against them and their followers. As we have seen, the labeling of the rivals as "Balaam" and "Jezebel" already expresses John's thoroughgoing denunciation of them and their teachings. Their teaching itself is called idolatry indirectly and harlotry directly. It is difficult to imagine two more emotionally laden concepts for the time and place, naturally in the negative sense. Christ is presented as saying that he *hates* the works of the Nicolaitans and as approving of the Ephesians' *hatred* of those works. The judgment Christ will execute on these unrepentant opponents is described in very violent terms, as we have seen.

In chapter 4 [of *Crisis and Catharsis*] I argued that the message to the Laodiceans (3:14–22) shows that John believed that under the circumstances Christians had to be at least detached from wealth, and that it was better to be economically poor. In chapter 3, Revelation 18 was interpreted as a condemnation of wealth obtained or held by collaboration with Roman power. In chapters 1 and 4, it was suggested that John was an itinerant prophet dependent on alms and hospitality. John's life and the book he wrote thus support that strand of early Christian tradition which is critical of wealth and idealizes poverty. As with the norm of exclusiveness, it seems that the implied idealization of poverty in Revelation has its origin in aggressive feeling, namely envy. We have seen how prominent gold, precious stones, pearls, and monumental architecture are in the vision of the new Jerusalem. In 5:12 it is proclaimed that the Lamb is worthy to receive power and wealth among other things. The Lamb's reception of them involves his followers too (5:10; 20:4–6; 21:24–26; 22:5). These elements show that wealth as such was not rejected in the Apocalypse. The problem was that the wrong people had power and wealth in John's situation. In order for the feeling of envy to be controlled, the possession of riches in the present had to be presented as evil and hateful in itself. This is done by linking wealth and pride: the Laodiceans are admonished as follows: "For you say, I am rich, I have prospered, and I need nothing; not knowing that you are wretched, pitiable, poor, blind, and naked" (3:17). More pointedly, Rome is accused of saying, "A queen I sit, I am no widow, mourning I shall never see" (18:7), in a context in which wealth is a major theme. It is also done by associating luxurious clothing and jewelry with drunkenness, harlotry, and even violence in the vision of "Babylon" in chapter 17. The list of cargo over which the wholesale dealers mourn consists, as we have seen, in large part of luxury items (18:11–13). The use of these goods is implicitly condemned by the subtle reproach of the last item: "bodies, that is, human souls" ("bodies" was the usual word for slaves).

In chapter 4, I argued that Revelation 14:4 idealizes continence. As shown in the same chapter, a high value was apparently placed on sexual continence from the beginning in some strands of Christian tradition. Nevertheless, the attitude reflected in Revelation may have been an intensification of norms in relation to Christian practice in the region at the time. This hypothesis is supported by the fact that continence is not advocated for all, but only for those who would "follow the Lamb wherever he goes." Once again, there is evidence of an origin in aggressive feeling. Continence is presented, not so much as a positive good, but rather as the avoidance of a disturbing alternative: "It is these who have not *defiled* themselves with women." Such a remark reveals a complex set of emotions, involving perhaps hatred and fear both of women and one's own body.

The Jewish writers Philo (first centuries B.C.E. and C.E.) and Josephus (first century C.E.) admired the Essenes for practicing continence. An intensified purity may well have been the Essenes' goal in the practice, but neither Philo nor Josephus emphasizes this rationale. Both of them speak of women in a highly stereotypical and misogynist way. Josephus comes closer to the idea of purity in saying that the Essenes avoid the danger of adultery by eschewing marriage. He also states that they renounced pleasure as evil and held resistance to the passions as a virtue.

It is clear that Josephus has reinterpreted the logic of purity in ethical terms. Both Josephus and Philo argued that the Essenes avoided marriage because the relationships between husband and wife and husband and children undermined the commitment to other members of the group essential for communal life. Josephus says simply that they believed marriage to lead to discord. Philo elaborates the idea at length.

John's presentation of continence in Revelation 14:4 is strictly in terms of purity. The particular form the ideal of purity takes here is rather extreme. No positive aspect of sexual intercourse is mentioned or implied. Josephus clearly respected the need for the propagation of the human race. The Gospel of Matthew recognized that intercourse was natural and in accordance with creation by speaking of the continent as eunuchs. There is no such ambiguity in Revelation. The hatred and fear of women apparently expressed in Revelation 14:4 probably have their roots in a negative attitude toward the body. Sexual intercourse and women are disturbing because they call to mind the vulnerability of a being with a body. Once again, an analogy with schizophrenia presents itself. According to Ernest Becker, the schizophrenic regards his or her body as something that "happened" to him or her. This attitude is simply a heightened awareness of something any human being might feel, as existentialist philosophers have shown. The schizophrenic views his or her body as a mass of stench and decay. This perspective is familiar also as the starting point of some forms of Buddhism. The schizophrenic takes this to an extreme, however, and feels that one's own body is only "a direct channel of vulnerability, the direct toehold that the outer world has on his [or her] most inner self. The body is his [or her] betrayal, his [or her] continually open wound, the object of his [or her] repulsion." I do not mean to imply that the remark in Revelation 14:4 rises out of a technically pathological situation. It is, however, a remark that demands critical assessment because of its potential for injustice toward women and alienation from the body.

The Book of Revelation is an important stage in the process toward the glorification of martyrdom in parts of the early church. This incipient attitude is expressed in the remark that the blood of those slain for their faith would be avenged when the number of those to be slain was complete (6:11). Some desirous of vengeance on Rome might have been led by such a remark to sacrifice themselves to the cause. The remark that the 144,000 are firstfruits to God and the Lamb suggests, by way of the metaphor of sacrifice, that they are witnesses by blood as well as by word. The implication is that those who died for the faith form an inner circle around the Lamb. The glorification of faithful death is most clear in the vision of the messianic reign (20:4–6). The urge to faithful death is obviously the most extreme form of the internalization of aggressive feeling and its reversal toward oneself.

CONCLUSION

Through the use of effective symbols and artful plots, the Apocalypse made feelings which were probably latent, vague, complex, and ambiguous explicit, conscious, and simple. Complex relationships were simplified by the use of a dualistic framework. The Jews who reject and denounce Christians are followers of Satan. Those who do not have God's seal bear the mark of the beast and are doomed to destruction. Fear, the sense of powerlessness, and aggressive feelings are not minimized, but heightened. They are placed in a cosmic framework, projected onto the screen of the heavenly world. This intensification leads to catharsis, a release of the disquieting elements of the emotions in question. By projecting the tension and the feelings experienced by the hearers into cosmic categories, the Apocalypse made it possible for the hearers to gain some distance from their experience. It provided a feeling of detachment and thus greater control.

Dedication to the rigors of exclusiveness, poverty, continence, and faithful death can be seen as the internalization of aggressive feelings aroused by social tensions. The practice of these intensified norms provided a way of releasing some of the energy aroused by those tensions. To a considerable extent, however, the aggressive feelings were not eliminated, but were transformed into new kinds of aggressive feeling. The resentment due to the hostility of Gentiles toward Christians was internalized in part by calling for greater exclusiveness. But the intensified norm of greater exclusiveness led to a division among Christians and aggressive feelings toward those who rejected or failed to live up to the intensified norm. A similar process may have occurred with regard to wealth. This transformation of aggression raises the question whether the process of containing aggression reflected in the Apocalypse is appropriate and adequate. It is certainly not dysfunctional or maladaptive in a pathological sense. It was adequate in the sense that pathological behavior was apparently avoided and, as far as we know, the anger of John and some hearers did not erupt into violence against their non-Christian neighbors, a violence that surely would have worsened their situation. The process was inadequate in the sense that the cause of aggressive feelings was not dealt with and resolved so that aggression could be eliminated without giving up on the ideal of a sociopolitical transformation. It is doubtful that a full resolution was possible, but more realistic attempts to solve the problem could have been formulated. Whether the process was appropriate is a question which involves theological and ethical reflection.

The Visionary Character: Revelation and the Lyrical Ballad

E. S. Shaffer

As a newly mythologized history encountered the Divine Word of the Bible, it released one set of epic possibilities; another more stunning and novel set of possibilities was released when the Word in its most symbolically extravagant and impenetrable form came into contact with the cutting edge of modern historical criticism. [Coleridge's projected] epic *Fall of Jerusalem* was not to be a history based on Josephus and rivalling Tasso, but the re-creation of a Book of Revelation in a time of reasoning doubt. As Carlyle proclaimed,

> Every man that writes is writing a new Bible; or a new Apocrypha; to last for a week or a thousand years; he that convinces a man and sets him working is the doer of a *miracle*.

The shape of romantic poetry, indeed poetry to the present day, begins to be visible as the eighteenth-century biblical epic emerges into the lyrical ballad.

Coleridge . . . was fully in agreement with the premises of the new biblical criticism. The first premise, that criticism could not shirk bringing the biblical accounts under the rational scrutiny of the new natural philosophy, had originated in a scathing attack from rationalists, deists, and sceptics on the whole range of supernatural claims made by and for the Bible. The second premise, that the Bible is to be approached like any other literary text, entailed the freedom to amend the "Holy Spirit" by establishing an accurate text, sifting the historical sources, questioning

From *"Kubla Khan"* and The Fall of Jerusalem: *The Mythological School in Biblical Criticism and Secular Literature, 1770–1880.* © 1975 by Cambridge University Press.

the traditional ascriptions of authorship and date, scrutinizing the formation of the canon, and comparing the Scriptures coolly with the sacred and secular writings of other nations. The significance of this procedure, whether or not it was openly stated in any given case, was simply the abandonment of the claim that the Bible is "inspired."

At the same time, however, the literary treatment of the Bible opened the way to a new apologetics of freethinking theism which was to salvage Christianity until very nearly the end of the Victorian era. It has been said that the higher criticism abolished traditional apologetics, only to establish a new apologetics vis-à-vis the Enlightenment. Coleridge's philosophical turn of mind led him to formulate the implications of the new criticism in the most general manner, and so made him both more radical than [Johann Gottfried] Eichhorn himself on several important issues and more sweepingly effective in creating a new apologetics. [Coleridge's own copy of Eichhorn's *Commentarius in Apocalypsin Johannis* contains extensive marginalia.]

The men who were prepared to apply the methods of secular literary criticism to the Bible were naturally quick to carry the results of their biblical criticism back into secular literature. The intricate interrelationship between *critica sacra* and *critica profana* in this period has never been traced. Yet its overwhelming importance for nineteenth-century literature has never ceased to be proclaimed.

To take one example: the Old Testament prophets and the apostles of the New were now to be considered as secular authors; yet were they not in some sense "inspired," though not literally dictated to by the Holy Spirit? What, then, is secular inspiration? This question came to focus in the figure of St John the Divine, the author of the Book of Revelation. The answer will give us an insight into the poet-seer with his "flashing eyes and floating hair," and how he governed the final form of "Kubla Khan."

Of all the books of the Old and the New Testament, the Book of Revelation had a peculiar aptness and fascination in the 1790s for a young poet of Coleridge's inclinations. Coleridge's great aim and accomplishment in criticism as in poetry was to refine and authenticate a form of the supernatural. The literature of his youth was dogged by rationalist explanations and exposures as crude and as sensational as the "Gothick" wonders and "graveyard" sensibilities that passed for supernatural. An alteration in sensibility could only be wrought by a revolution in religious attitudes as well as in poetic modes. To poetize this book was to attempt the heights of Miltonic sublimity from a perspective dictated by the boldest results of criticism.

Milton, in the famous passage in *The Reason of Church Government* in which he reviewed the poetic genres of the Bible, including Job as the model of the "brief epic," and "the divine pastoral drama" in the Song of Solomon, spoke impressively of the Apocalypse:

> And the Apocalypse of Saint John is the majestick image of a high and stately Tragedy, shutting up and intermingling her solemn Scenes and Acts with a sevenfold Chorus of halleluja's and harping symphonies.

Not only does the enterprise of setting Revelation to poetry have the *imprimatur* of Milton, the highest of all authorities for the young poet Coleridge, but he envisages it in terms which suggest a wholly different approach from the neoclassical. If the versifying of the Bible according to neoclassical precepts was hedged about with dire warnings against the falsification of history and the mishandling of sacred doctrine, there was a longer tradition whereby biblical poetry benefited not only from the solemnity of its subject but from a special freedom to invest a variety of genres. Biblical poetry in the eighteenth century was still able to accomplish the renovation and innovation of genres. It is in this sense that we may understand the words of Girard: "L'épopée religieuse a été le grand rêve romantique."

The solemnity and weight of biblical poetry were not owing to its sacredness only. The Alexandrian allegorical exegesis taken over by Christian apologists had located all knowledge whatsoever in the Bible. If this practice began as a defence against the superiority of pagan Greek learning in the Hellenistic world, the doctrine of the correspondence between secular and sacred wisdom became, by the time of Isidore of Seville's *Etymologiae,* an imperious claim for Israel's primacy in philosophy, science, and poetry, maintained, like the claim for literal historical primacy, well into the eighteenth century.

Thus, it was said, Genesis and Ecclesiastes are compendia of physics; ethics is summed up in the Proverbs of Solomon; in Job are to be found "all the laws of dialectics"; and all of logic is set out in the Song of Songs, possibly the most astonishing of all the astonishing claims to be made for the Song of Songs. Coleridge's *The Statesman's Manual* contains an only slightly more moderate contemporary variation on the theme: "All the important truths and efficient practical directions of Thucydides, Tacitus, Machiavelli, Bacon and Harrington preexist in the Bible": and their "particular rules and precepts flow directly and visibly from universal principles, as from a fountain."

The old view that the Bible contained all wisdom paradoxically took on new life through the historical-critical movement, for again all knowledge was brought to bear on it, and all human religious experience was to be found in it, not merely the special revelation of Christianity. Thus [J. G. von] Herder wrote to [J. G.] Hamann:

> Die "magere" Bibel wird all sieben Wissenschaften der alten und tausend der neuen Welt wie die fetten Kühe Pharaos in sich schlucken, bis ein Tag kommt, der durch Facta und Acta alles entsiegelt.

> (The "lean" Bible will swallow all seven arts of the old world and a thousand of the new like the fat kine of Pharaoh, until a day comes that unseals all things in Facta and Acta.)

No lean book of the Bible was better suited to become a Pharaonic cow, or a Trojan horse, of the new and the old knowledge than Revelation, which traditionally "unsealed" the mysteries of the old world and a new to the eyes of the seer.

The Book of Revelation seemed to clamour for a free, an "anticlassical," treatment. Older models for such a Revelation epic were the panoramic poems of the Patristic poets and the celestial cycle poems like Du Bartas's *Sepmaine,* treating the seven days of creation, and his unfinished second *Sepmaine* presenting the seven ages of man's restoration, Tasso's own *Il mondo creato,* and the epics of the three-phase celestial cycles that Milton drew on. Within the biblical epic certain techniques grew up for both overcoming and taking advantage of formlessness. The earliest Christian manoeuvre, the typological interpretation of the Old Testament, whereby principal characters and events foreshadow their "counterparts" in the New, made for great flexibility in time schemes, which was further extended by the Patristic adoption of the Virgilian prophetic dream and vision of the future, from then on a standard feature of biblical epic. Typology succeeded in subordinating not only Old Testament, but also classical heroes to New Testament significance. As a whole series of Old Testament children—Abel, Isaac, Joseph, Samson—might be represented as types of Christ, so a variety of classical figures historical and fictional—the Curii, Socrates, Hercules—could equally well be types of Christ. Like typological linking, the dream-vision was particularly popular in the Middle Ages, and a striking epic example is the *Northern Passion* of the fourteenth century, which incorporated the matter of the Book of Revelation into the Passion story as a vision seen by John when he reclined on Christ's bosom at the Last Supper. Indeed, the Book of Revelation can be taken as the climax and summation of the typological method, for coming at the end of the Bible it may be held to resume the whole structure, so that to unravel its symbols is to set before one the entire cycle from the division in heaven, to the creation of the world and the fall of man, to the reunion with the divine.

By the eighteenth century, biblical poetry had attained a greater degree of freedom than even these epics enjoy. The necessity of finding formal elements outside the Bible had always been a source of freedom, for despite the claim that the Bible was the original of all forms, the poets, trained in the classics, looked even in the Bible for classical genres. The formlessness of the Bible by classical standards made it possible to impose almost any one of the panoply of classical forms on any book of the Bible.

Coleridge indulges in the sport:

> It is quite wonderful, that Luther who could see so plainly that Judith was an Allegoric Poem should have been blind to the Book of Jonas being an Apologue, in which Jonas means the Israelitish nation!

The two most popular parts of the Old Testament, the Song of Songs and the Book of Job, were treated as "models"—that is, as fit materials to have other forms imposed upon them—of an extraordinary range of genres. The Book of Job was sometimes thought of as a regular Greek tragedy. Milton, of course, considered it as the model of the "brief epic." [Robert] Lowth devoted considerable space to arguing that it was not a classical tragedy: "The Greeks would have called such a production a Monody, or Elegiac Dialogue, or anything but a tragedy" (*Lectures on the Sacred Poetry of the Hebrews*). By then it sufficed as an accolade to call it simply the "most sublime" of Hebrew poems.

Even more startling are the transformations undergone by the Song of Songs. Origen himself wrote a dramatic version of it. Bernard of Clairvaux's allegorical interpretation is one of the most brilliant works of the Middle Ages. Milton called it "a divine pastoral drama." In the eighteenth century, Herder, freed from classical genres by his comprehension of Hebrew poetry, broke new ground by considering it simply as a series of sensuous love songs, "weltliche Liebeslieder," unconnected dramatically or allegorically, "eine Reihe schöner Perlen auf eine Schnur gefasset," "a series of lovely pearls strung on one thread." In 1775 Goethe did a translation in this spirit. At the time of the *West-östlicher Divan,* he still held that no connection could be found between "these fragments." But after the appearance in 1820 of K. F. Umbreit's translation and commentary, he described the connection once more as "dramatic"; "Und so löst sich der epische Unzusammenhang doch in einem Zusammenhange auf," "And so epic disconnectedness resolves itself after all into a unity."

Coleridge similarly reshuffled the genres. He seems originally to have regarded the poem as an epithalamium on the marriage of Solomon to an Egyptian princess, a simple love poem; but later returned to the view that it signified the Messiah's communion with the soul.

The Bible, then, had always been a source for poetic genres, and lent itself to differing interpretations according to the popularity of certain genres at different times. The Sacred Writings, the literal Word of God, curiously became the most malleable of materials. No form, but an inspired formlessness, an infinite potentiality of form, or capacity to assume all forms, is suggested by the tradition of biblical poetry.

The lyric poetry of the Bible, Milton had said in the passage in which he spoke of the Apocalypse, can rival the "magnifick Odes and Hymns" of Pindar and Callimachus. With the introduction of the ode form late in the sixteenth century had emerged the figure of the inspired "Pindaric" bard. In England, the Old Testament David the Harpist was quickly established as the poetic equal of the great classical odists. The Protestant hymnody of the Reformation adopted first the Old Testament psalms; the new Greek scholarship encouraged the many metrical translations of the Psalms of David, culminating, in England, in the classical humanist version of George Sandys in 1643. The new *Textkritik* of the Bible followed the same path, comparing first the New Testament Greek with classical Greek texts, and then moving on into Jewish-Hellenistic literature and, in John Lightfoot's work on the Gospels (1658–78), into the study of biblical Hebrew. On this parallelism of Greek and Hebrew culture Milton built, accomplishing the first phase of poetic Orientalism.

Milton's *Samson Agonistes* combines tragedy with a sublime lyric art aspiring to outdo the Greek, and the preface to *Samson* describes the Book of Revelation as a precedent:

> Pareus, commenting on the Revelation, divides the whole book
> as a tragedy, into acts, distinguished each by a Chorus of heav-
> enly harpings and songs between.

The lyrical freedom won for biblical poetry was exploited by [Friedrich Gottlieb] Klopstock, the best of Milton's eighteenth-century imitators. His fine prose tragedy *Der Tod Adams, The Death of Adam,* versified in its English translation, is less a drama than an extended ode to death. In the *Messias,* he came close to combining the Miltonic epic with the Miltonic choric tragedy. As the theorist of "heilige Poesie," "sacred poetry," and a first-rate practitioner of the ode form, he adapted *geistliche Gesänge,* "spiritual songs," to the purposes of the blank-verse hexameter epic. The actual events of the Passion being brief and iconographical, it is presented as a series of vast invocations, prophecies, visions, cosmic and individual prayers of praise, denunciations, lamentations, and seraphic rejoicings.

Klopstock was the champion of the possibility of a "Protestant mythology" in poetry, and Coleridge sympathized with this, although he was able in practice to remove the note of sectarian controversy:

> Are the "innumerable multitude of angels & archangels" less splendid beings than the countless Gods & Goddesses of Rome & Greece?—And can you seriously think that Mercury from Jove equals in poetic sublimity "the mighty Angel that came down from Heaven, whose face was as it were the Sun, and his feet as pillars of fire: Who set his right foot on the sea, and his left upon the earth. And he sent forth a loud voice; and when he had sent it forth, seven Thunders uttered their Voices: and when the seven Thunders had uttered their Voices, the mighty Angel lifted up his hand to Heaven, & sware by Him that liveth for ever & ever, that TIME was no more?" (Rev. 10, 1–6) Is not Milton a *sublimer* poet than Homer or Virgil? Are not his Personages more sublimely cloathed? And do you not know, that there is not perhaps *one* page in Milton's Paradise Lost, in which he has not borrowed his imagery from the *Scriptures?*—I allow, and rejoice that *Christ* appealed only to the understanding & the affections; but I affirm that, after reading Isaiah or St Paul's Epistle to the Hebrews, Homer & Virgil are disgustingly *tame* to me, & Milton himself barely tolerable.
>
> (Letter to Thelwall, December 17, 1796)

In view of the shape-shifting of biblical texts in the direction of the lyric, it is hardly surprising that even Eichhorn's outline of the acts and scenes of the "grand prophetic drama" of the Fall of Jerusalem, despite the euhemerizing commentary that follows, reads much more like Milton's "seven-fold Chorus of halleluja's and harping symphonies" than like a dramatic action:

The Drama Itself

PRELUDE c. iv–c. viii. 5.
> The Scene is set.
> (a) God is seen sitting upon the throne. c. iv. 1–11.
> (b) Jesus Christ is seen enthroned with God and in addition a volume containing future changes of things sealed in letters, and at the same time it is declared, no one but God and his companion on the throne knows the argument of the volume. c. v. 1–14. . . .
> (e) The horror of the omens increases, portending evils to the adversaries of the Christian religion. c. vi. 12–17. . . .

ACT I c. viii. 6–c. xii. 17.
Jerusalem falls, or Judaism is conquered by the Christian Religion
> (a) Public calamity is prophesied. c. viii. 6–12.
Conclusion. The triple woe is proclaimed. c. viii. 13. . . .

ACT II c. xii. 18–c. xx. 10.
Rome falls, or the Gentiles are conquered by the Christian religion. . . .
> Rome, the seat of idolatry, is described under the image of a sea monster, in order that an idea of idolatry should be excited in the souls of the readers. c. xii. 18–c. xiii. 10.
> The preceding scene is set with another monster emerging from the earth which counterfeits the prophet, who, having arranged prodigies and miracles to deceive mankind, aids the sea-monster. c. xii. 11–18.
Conclusion. The happiness of the worshippers of God and the contented state and condition of their souls is contrasted with the rage of the profane Gentiles and tumult of spirit with which they burn. c. xiv. 1–5. . . .
> Rome at last falls. c. xvi. 17–21. . . .
> (c) Lament over conquered Rome. c. xviii. 1–24.

(d) Triumphal song. c. xix. 1–10.

(e) Triumphal march. c. xix. 11–c. xx. 3. . . .

ACT III c. xx. 11–c. xxii. 5.

The heavenly Jerusalem descends from the sky, or the bliss of future life which will endure forever is described.

(a) The scene is set: namely, the dead are resurrected and honest men are assembled among the citizens of the heavenly republic. c. xx. 11–14.

(b) The New Jerusalem, seat of the rule of the Messiah and of the happiness of future life is described. c. xxi. 1–c. xxii. 5.

The Book of Revelation, then, constituted the ultimate challenge to the writer of sublime poetry, to the bard aspiring to equal Pindar and David, and appeared so even in the hands of the soberest historical critic.

But what would be the character of an apocalyptic poem? If the Book of Revelation was the most sublime book of the Bible, it was also the most nearly uncanonical, the most suspect, the most questionable. It had been the first biblical text (apart from the Pauline epistles) to be attacked by the early Fathers as unapostolic, and on literary grounds that were to be developed fully by the higher criticism, and most especially by Herder and by Coleridge himself. It could the more easily be breached: Eichhorn felt able to publish his commentary on it more than a decade before he dared approach the public with his work on the Gospels.

Moreover, the book's holiness was as heretical as its fraudulence. Its visionary character had rendered it a particular favourite of the extreme Protestant sects and those who like Boehme claimed a similar gift. To this day the standard Christian authorities are silent concerning a vast, subterranean, mystical, and sometimes half-mad literature of interpretation that fed on hermetic and cabalistic sources and still flourishes in a variety of pseudoscientific forms. Even those uses of it which were to become orthodox, the visions of the New Jerusalem in Protestant hymns, took root first in the sectarian fringes of Puritanism and in the Herrnhüter and finally in Wesleyanism. If Isaac Watts's hymns and John Wesley's translations from the Herrnhüter *Gesangbuch* now reside in Anglican hymnals, their development in Blake reminds us of the powerful idiosyncrasy of that Protestant claim to literal vision which rejoiced in the New Jerusalem:

There is a land of pure Delight,
    Where Saints immortal reign;
Infinite Day excludes the Night,
    And Pleasures banish Pain.

There everlasting Spring abides,
    And never-withering Flowers;
Death like a narrow Sea divides
    This Heav'nly Land from ours.

Sweet Fields beyond the swelling Flood
    Stand drest in living Green:
So to the *Jews* old Canaan stood,
    While *Jordan* roll'd between.

The Book of Revelation lent itself with particular pyrotechnical ease to the eighteenth-century conception of the epic as sacred song. At the same time, its purported author became the focus of the investigation of the nature of prophetic inspiration and the authenticity of the biblical canon. Could John the Apostle, John the Evangelist, and John the Apocalyptic have been the same man? If not, what was the basis of the author's authority, and, by extension, of the canonical authority of the Book of Revelation and indeed of the Fourth Gospel?

Once again, it had been Herder who had begun to consider the Old Testament prophets not as receptacles of divine inspiration, but as men with a special gift for evoking the numinous; and all that Herder had enthusiastically suggested, Eichhorn converted into the hermeneutic norm. In the 1790s their analysis touched the New Testament; as Christianity lost its claim to a unique revelation, the apostles themselves could be seen as prophet-poets, as bards of an antique saga. As the dating and the historical analysis of the contents of the Gospels proceeded, John was set apart from the three newly labelled "synoptic" Gospel writers, as reflecting a Hellenistic, philosophized account of the original Judaic saga. The traditional fondness for John as the young apostle who was Jesus's favourite merges oddly but impressively with his new importance as the carrier of pagan conceptions into the mainstream of Christianity. In John, the antique bard evolved into the sophisticated conscious poet; John became the New Testament equivalent of Pindar and David. John the Apocalyptic absorbed the new intensity of the Evangelist's image; and the scepticism attaching to his own identity, and therefore to his prophetic capacity, increased the ambiguous attractions and the poetic range of

"John." In the context of biblical criticism, the strange conjunction of the especially holy and the especially heretical that had always characterized the Book of Revelation was carried over decisively into the romantic seer. In the familiar yet uncanny figure of the holy man of "Kubla Khan" we have one of the very first of a long line of apostles of poetry.

Herder's antisupernatural view of prophecy, his Hebraic "humanism," was prefigured in literature, as the new biblical criticism was to have in turn a striking effect on literature. In Klopstock's *Messias,* the Book of Revelation is incorporated into the figure of the visionary apostle John, the most prominent and vivid person—perhaps the only person—in the poem, and indispensable to its theology: as Jesus is the merciful mediator between God and man, so John is the merciful mediator between the Son of God and man. The young friend of Jesus, like Goethe's Iphigenia, is the image of the humane, civilized man of feeling. It is precisely his humanity that makes him the beloved of Christ and opens to him the visionary experiences denied to the other apostles. This somewhat surprising collocation follows from Klopstock's treatment of prophecy as rational event, Coleridge's objections to which we have already noted. According to Klopstock, if John is seen as fully human, then his visions, being rationalized at their source, can be as extravagant as the poet pleases. But just as when he presents miracle as "fact," so when he presents human feeling as prophetic, the gap is not narrowed but widened between nature and supernature. In the context of individual psychology, moreover, the technique works much more successfully than in a "factual" fantasy of the miraculous. It is not the doubting audience that is witness to the vision in history, but John, and his credible human sentiments and tender susceptibility render his visions comprehensible and genuine, although they are in no sense self-induced, or "psychological" in a modern sense. The technique works so well that the reader more than once wishes that Klopstock had imagined the whole of his epic through John's eyes. But in the epic tradition the inspired poet narrated events from outside the poem; he did not sing them from within. Klopstock still claimed objectivity of vision both for the bard and for the visionary character.

The first scene with John is the highpoint of that graveyard poetry over which Klopstock waxed so enthusiastic, holding up "the prophet" Young's *Nächte* as his great model after Milton. Unaccountable as this enthusiasm for the *Night-Thoughts* may seem to the English reader, we see here what could be made of it.

In Book 1 and the opening of Book 2 (in heaven) the imagery of light and dark has already been established on a cosmic scale. Jesus is first seen alone on the Mount of Olives, as the souls of Adam and Eve pray to Him for mercy for the human race.

> Jesus vernahm sie
> Fern in der Tiefe. Wie mitten in heiligen Einsiedleyen,
> In der Zukunft Folge vertieft, prophetische Weise
> Dich, in der fern herwandelnde Stimme des Ewigen, hören.

(The Messiah heard them in his deep recess, as in a sacred solitude, the holy prophet rapt in contemplation, hears, in soft whispers, the voice of the Eternal.)

He descends, seeking John. Raphael describes to Him how John in his sleep had visions of Jesus, and tells Him where to find John: among the sepulchres of human bones, caring for a man possessed by grief. Jesus, touched by Raphael's description of John as the type of humanity, approaches "den Gräbern der Toten," the tombs of the dead.

> Unten am mitternächtlichen Berge waren die Gräber
> In zusammengebirgte zerrüttete Felsen gehauen.
> Dicke, finsterverwachsene Wälder verwahrten den Eingang,
> Vor des fliehenden Wandrers Blick. Ein trauriger Morgen
> Stieg, wenn der Mittag schon sich über Jerusalem senkte,
> Dämmernd noch in die Gräber mit kühlem Schauer hinunter.

(Jesus now drew near to the sepulchres hewn in the cliff of the rock, where thick and gloomy woods guarded the entrance from the view of the hasty traveller. Here the morning dawn lowered in chilly coolness, and the sun faintly shot his beams among the tombs.)

The terrible episode follows in which the "possessed" man Samma kills his youngest and favourite son by dashing him against the cliff, and is overwhelmed again by his own grief. We recognize the world of Wordsworth's "Guilt and Sorrow" and "The Mad Mother." Jesus restores Samma:

> Ins bleiche Gesicht voll Todesgestalten
> Kam die Menschheit zurück, er schrie, und weinte gen
> Himmel.

(Life [in an earlier version, "Humanität"] dawns in that face,

which just before had the awful stamp of death. With a loud
cry and streaming eyes, he looks towards heaven.)

The remaining son turns to John to ask that he and his healed father
be permitted to follow the prophet Jesus. Jesus dismisses them gently,
and remains with John among the graves of man, until later the apostles
seek Jesus as night falls and the threats to His life increase.

Again at the Last Supper Jesus vouchsafes a vision to John, the only
one of the disciples to see it, and again this is the direct result of his
humanity. Jesus passed the bread and the sacred cup:

> Da Johannes sich naht, und auf den glänzenden Kelch sah,
> Warf er zu Jesus Füssen sich nieder, küsste die weinend,
> Trocknete dann die Thränen mit seiner fallenden Locke,
>   Lass ihn meine Herrlichkeit sehn! sprach Jesus und schaute
> Zu dem Vater empor. Johannes erhub sich, und sahe
> In der Tiefe des Saals der Seraphim helle Versammlung.
> Und die Seraphim wüssten, dass er sie sahe. Johannes
> Stand in Entzückung verloren. Er schaute Gabriels Hoheit
> Starr, mit Erstaunen. Er schaute des himmlischen Raphael
>   Glänzen.
> Und verehrt ihn. Er sah auch Salem in menschlichem
>   Schimmer,
> Und mit ausgebreiteten Armen entgegen ihm lächeln;
> Und er liebte den Seraph. Er wandte sich um, und erblickte
> In des Messias rühigem Auge die Spuren der Gottheit;
> Und er sank verstümmend ans Herz des erhabnen Messias.

(When John, seized with a sudden transport, sunk down at
his feet, kissed them, and wetted them with his tears.

Jesus then, looking up towards heaven, with a gracious
smile, cried, O Father! permit him to see my glory. John then
arising beheld at the end of the chamber a bright assembly of
angels, who knew that he saw them. Rapt in an ecstatic transport, he beheld the sublime Gabriel, with motionless astonishment: enraptured he saw the brightness of the celestial
Raphael, and him he honoured: with delight unutterable, he
also perceived Salem in an human form, who with a smile of
friendship, opened his arms, and him he loved. Now, turning
his ravished eyes, he discovered in the Messiah's placid coun-

tenance ["Auge"], traces of his celestial glory, and sunk speechless on his bosom.)

John's traditional pose in Jesus' arms is here the direct and immediate result of his having been overcome by a vision of Christ's glory. Vision and human love are inextricable. The intense preference for John over the other apostles in this contemporary form passed over, through [Gotthold Ephraim] Lessing and Herder, into biblical criticism. The process by which the evangelists became antique Oriental bards, and John the philosophic and poetic genius among them, is as complex as it is fascinating.

John was brought into special prominence by the investigation of the order and mutual relations of the four Gospels. J. D. Michaelis, whose *Einleitung in das Neue Testament, Introduction to the New Testament,* Coleridge read in translation in 1795, denied the mutual dependence of the three first Gospels, and attributed their similarities to a common use of "anderer apocryphische Evangelia," "other apocryphal Gospels," that is, he originated the idea that behind the existing Gospels stood an earlier text or texts. Lessing, in one of his *Kleine Schriften,* "Theses aus der Kirchengeschichte," "Theses from Ecclesiastical History," published only after his death, suggested that the *Urevangelium* or archetypal Gospel standing behind the three first Gospels was the Aramaic gospel of the heretical Jewish Christians (Nazarenes) reported by the church fathers. By tracing the synoptic gospels to a heretical Jewish original, Lessing increased the value of the Gospel of John. It was John who had rescued the Gospel out of the hands of an ephemeral Jewish sect and made it worthy to be the basis of a world religion:

> Nur sein Evangelium gab der christlichen Religion ihre wahre Konsistenz; nur seinem Evangelio haben wir es zu danken, wenn die christliche Religion in dieser Konsistenz allen An-fällen ungeachtet noch fortdauert und vermutlich so lange fort-dauern wird, als es Menschen gibt, die eines Mittlers zwischen ihnen und der Gottheit zu bedürfen glauben; das ist ewig.

> (Only his Gospel gave the Christian religion its true consistency; we have his Gospel alone to thank if the Christian religion in this consistency still endures in spite of all onslaughts and continues to endure as we suppose it will as long as there are human beings who believe that they require a mediator between them and divinity; that is eternal.)

Eichhorn carried out Michaelis's suggestion more fully, and it is usually with his name that the *Urevangeliumshypothese* is associated. Eichhorn's attempt to go behind the existing documents had the effect of throwing interest back on the earliest historical conditions of primitive Christianity. Much of what the Gospels told of Jesus consisted of mere "sagas," he held, late accretions drawn from pre-Christian legendary material.

If Eichhorn showed a certain rationalist contempt for sagas and legends, Herder fell on the suggestion enthusiastically. He agreed with Lessing that the *Jesubild* of the synoptic Gospels was at odds with that of John, and that John was incomparably superior in literary value and theological sophistication. But he was prepared to accord the earlier Evangelists special value as primitive poets of the new religion. The oldest Gospel was Jesus' own preaching, and the apostles, like rhapsodes ("evangelische Rhapsoden"), composed out of their witness not a written Gospel, but an oral one, that gradually grew into a cycle, held in common by the community. He criticized his colleagues for applying the notions of a bookish age to the primitive unlettered society of the earliest Christians, and he analysed the style of the Gospels in terms of primitive bardic poetry:

> *Bei einer freien mündlichen Erzählung ist nicht alles gleich frei.* Sentenzen, grosse Aussprüche, Parabeln erhalten sich eher in demselben Ausdruck, als kleine Umstände der Geschichte; Übergänge und Bindungsformeln wählet der Erzählende selbst. In unsern Evangelien ist dieser Unterschied klar. Gewisse, insonderheit starke, dunkle, parabolische Ausdrücke sind allenthalben, selbst mit verschiedener Deutung, dieselben; in Umständen, in Übergängen, in Ordnung der Begebenheiten gehen die Erzählungen am freisten aus einander. . . .
>
> *Das gemeinsame Evangelium bestand aus einzelnen Stücken, Erzählungen, Parabeln, Sprüchen, Perikopen.* Dies gibt die Ansicht der Evangelien selbst und die verschiedene Ordnung, in der diese und jene Parabel oder Sage gesetzt ist. . . . Es bürgt für die Wahrheit des Evangeliums, dass es aus solchen Theilen bestehet: denn Leute, wie die meisten Apostel waren, erinnerten sich leichter eines Spruches, einer Parabel, eines Apophthegma, das ihnen auffallend gewesen war, als zusammenhängender Reden.
>
> (*In a free oral narrative not everything is equally free.* Maxims,

great sayings, parables are more easily retained in the same form of expression than trivial details of history: transitions and connecting formulas the narrator chooses himself. In our Gospels this difference is clear. Certain particularly strong, dark, parabolic expressions are everywhere the same, even when they have various meanings; in circumstantial detail, in transitions, in the ordering of events the Gospel narratives depart from one another most freely. . . .

The common Gospel consisted of separate pieces, stories, parables, sayings, pericopes. This is clear from the form of the Gospels themselves and from the differing order in which this and that parable or saga is placed. It is a guarantee of the truth of the Gospel that it consists of such fragments: for common people, as most of the apostles were, were better able to remember a saying, a parable, an apothegm than logically consistent speeches.)

Although Herder agreed that John was superior both as theology and as literature to the other evangelists, he regarded these merits as derived from and developing the special qualities of the primitive bardic cycle. It was precisely the legendary basis of saga that made the Gospels a testament of faith rather than a chronicle of the biographical facts of the life of Jesus, and therefore opened the way for John's philosophical treatment of the legendary material:

Überhaupt beweiset das Evangelium Johannes die Idee am besten, . . . dass sie die Evangelien nämlich auf keine Weise Biographieen, sondern historische Beurkundungen des christlichen Glaubensbekenntnisses seyn sollten, das Jesus der Christ sey, und wie er es gewesen. Johannes Evangelium, als das späteste, verfolgt diesen Zweck im bestimmtesten Umriss; eine eigentliche Biographie verliert man dabei ganz aus dem Augen, an welche man auch, als Hauptidee derselben betrachtet, bei den ältern Evangelien nicht denken sollte. Sie sind, was ihr Name saget.

(The Gospel of John offers by far the best proof of the idea . . . that the Gospels were not meant in any sense as biographies, but as historical witnesses to the Christian faith that Jesus was the Christ, and in the manner described. John's Gospel, as the latest in date, pursues this aim most firmly; it banishes all notions of an actual biography, as indeed, even in the earlier Gospels, the leading idea ought never to be thought of as biographical. The Gospels are, what their name conveys.)

In Herder's formulation, there was no longer any need to choose between the virtues of the primitive cycle and the virtues of the sophisticated, self-conscious version of it; the sophisticated bard unfolded more fully and theoretically, although in the same "dark" style, what the primitive bard had indispensably envisioned. The opposites of primitive and sophisticate, of naive and sentimental, were reconciled in the figure of the poet-prophet John. "John" represents a solution to Herder's lifelong attempts to define the primitive state in such a way that it clearly denoted the highest poetic quality.

Coleridge, following rather than initiating these developments, took an independent course through them. He too regarded both the Old Testament prophets and the New Testament evangelists as bards. In his *Confessions of an Enquiring Spirit, or Letters on the Inspiration of the Scriptures,* he subscribed with a fullness of enthusiasm that outdoes even Herder to the poetic inspiration of the bard David:

> But let me once be persuaded that all these heart-awakening utterances of human hearts—of men of like faculties and passions with myself, mourning, rejoicing, suffering, triumphing—are but as a *Divina Commedia* of a superhuman—Oh bear with me, if I say—Ventriloquist;—that the royal Harper, to whom I have so often submitted myself as a *many-stringed instrument* for his fire-tipt fingers to traverse, while every several nerve of emotion, passion, thought, that thrids the flesh-and-blood of our common humanity, responded to the touch,— that this *sweet Psalmist of Israel* was himself as mere an instrument as his harp, an *automaton* poet, mourner, and suppli-cant;—all is gone,—all sympathy, at least, and all example.

Vigorous defence of the bardic abilities of prophetic Orientals was encouraged by enlightened sneers at the Pentateuch as an "Arabian tale." Coleridge held that the first eleven chapters of Exodus are "of a later date, a distinct book, a traditional Life of Moses and his brother Aaron" and that they were compiled by the "Rhapsodi, or Homerenoumenoi, the Bards or Prophets" who collected the cycle of war songs or ballads "rudely organized in the Historical Book of Judges."

In his willingness to attribute the Books of Moses and other parts of the Old Testament to a series of bards and interpolators, Coleridge was more radical than Eichhorn. Eichhorn refused, through the four editions of his book, to entertain the idea that the Pentateuch was not all of a piece (though it might have been written by "the Deuteronomist" rather than Moses); this has been accounted the major block in his Old Testament scholarship.

Coleridge may well have been better prepared than Eichhorn to entertain the most radical hypothesis about the Pentateuch, for this had been an English speciality since Hobbes had first suggested in *Leviathan* that the Books of Moses were not by but about Moses. He was of course familiar with Spinoza's attribution of the Pentateuch to Ezra. Moreover, from at least 1792 Coleridge was familiar with Geddes's "Fragment-Hypothesis": the Pentateuch did not merely draw on earlier sources, but was put together by an editor out of a collection of independent and often conflicting fragments.

The terms in which Coleridge puts his acceptance of the fragmentation, however, show how thoroughly he had absorbed Herder's notion of the communal experience as a unifying element. Thus he agreed with Eichhorn that interpolations in the Book of Daniel during the tyranny of Antiochus Epiphanes made it a "political Pamphlet" and, as the deist Anthony Collins had pointed out, not prophecy at all; but this in no way detracts from the authenticity of the Book, for the interpolations were made by "men of genius" among the Maccabees who employed "floating legends" well-known in the Jewish community and equivalent to ours of "Merlin, Nostradamus, etc. and the Greeks and Romans of the Sibyls."

Coleridge was prepared to multiply interpolations, and to defend them, where Eichhorn denied them. On Genesis 36:31 he remarked:

> But why *not* consider this as a gloss introduced by the Editors of the Pentateuch, or Preparers of the Copy that was to be layed up in the Temple of Solomon? The authenticity of the Books would be no more compromised by such glosses, than that of the Book before me by this marginal Note of mine.

In short, such additions, as long as they are indigenous, actually add to the Bible's value as a record of the community, political and folkloric as well as religious.

For Coleridge, this view of the Pentateuch banished the orthodox claim to the literal inspiration of the New Testament as well, for the doctrine of absolute inspiration, of supernatural dictation or theopneusty, was derived, he wrote, from the Rabbis, who "confined this miraculous character to the Pentateuch. Between the Mosaic and the Prophetic inspiration they asserted such a difference as amounts to a diversity."

In the same way, he was more radical than Eichhorn about the documentary backing for the Gospels. He agreed with Eichhorn, against Schleiermacher, that there was some documentary backing from apostolic times for the Gospels as finally formulated in the second century (he may not have known Schleiermacher on Luke until he annotated Thirlwall's translation in 1825). He did not, however, admit an *Urevangelium* in the literal sense of a manuscript drawn on by the writers of the Gospels, but sophisticated it rather through a Herderian conception of a community of oral, legendary material that helped shape the primary documents as well as the Gospels.

The New Testament like the Old Testament was a "cycle" which was held in common by the members of the primitive community, and which could always be added to or revised in the light of new circumstances. The flexibility of the text under primarily oral conditions is appropriately transferred to the critical interpretation when the text becomes fixed in literate times. The piecemeal, traditional, inconsistent character of the text, and its construction out of mobile "elements," is precisely the mark of its essential wholeness, its ability to maintain its most general purposes through no matter how much alteration of specific parts.

Nothing could better illustrate Coleridge's admiration for "John" as the New Testament bard than his early attempts to poetize the Book of Revelation in the style of Klopstock:

> And blest are they,
> Who in this fleshly World, the elect of Heaven,
> Their strong eye darting through the deeds of men,
> Adore with steadfast unpresuming gaze
> Him Nature's essence, mind, and energy!
> And gazing, trembling, patiently ascend
> Treading beneath their feet all visible things
> As steps, that upward to their Father's throne
> Lead gradual—else nor glorified nor loved.
> They not contempt embosom nor revenge:
> For they dare know of what may seem deform
> The Supreme Fair sole operant: in whose sight
> All things are pure, his strong controlling love
> Alike from all educing perfect good.
> Their's too celestial courage, inly armed—

> Dwarfing Earth's giant brood, what time they muse
> On their great Father, great beyond compare!
> And marching onwards view high o'er their heads
> His waving banners of Omnipotence.
>
> ("Religious Musings")

Herder made his own passionate attempt at conveying the style of "John":

> He who has eyes to see, or who is possessed of any genuine
> feeling, will trace in the apocalypse the same prevailing fea-
> tures which distinguish the Gospel. . . . [T]he spirit which
> pervades it, is, after all, the greatest text. If I were to describe
> the writings of St. John, I should say they shewed a soul both
> strong and tender; an amiable anxiety to be perspicuous; a
> peculiar gift for leading his reader by the slightest indication;
> strong masses of light and shade; economy, and at the same
> time copiousness, of imagery; a constant recurrence to the
> main thought, through the slender threads with which it is
> insensibly connected. His Gospel is pregnant with poetical
> simplicity, and varies with most significant emblems. In the
> one you see the eagle, soaring to the sun; in the other you have
> the dove, with all its native mildness. The Revelations are like
> the royal aloe, pre-eminent above plants. The Gospel is the
> lily and the rose, streaked with the blood of affection: the least
> word conveys the sentiment to the heart.
>
> (A Brief Commentary on the Revelation of Saint John)

Neither Herder's rhetorical description of the style nor Coleridge's
attempt to reproduce it comes very near the mark; but their aspiration,
at least, is clear. It is, indeed, the John of the Apocalypse who seems to
fuse the Apostle and the Evangelist, and so sets a stylistic standard impossible to achieve: he sees both the historical milieu of Jesus and the
milieu of the philosophized history of the Fourth Gospel as one visionary
landscape. Herder's *Blätter* on contemporary poetry contain a lively dialogue between a Christian and a Rabbi, under the heading "Christian
poems in oriental taste (Klopstock)"—notice the classification of Klopstock's New Testament epic *Messias* as "Oriental"—in which the Rabbi
complains that Klopstock has no sense whatsoever for the Jewish milieu
of Jesus, and the Christian defends Klopstock on the equally historical
grounds that the *Messias* is "a song of the origin of our religion." From
the Christian point of view, it is quite right not to depict the realistic

historical milieu as it was known to contemporary Jews, but the "myth-ological" milieu of the Gospels, the milieu of belief.

The Christian reinforces his point by exclaiming:

> Hätte unser Johannes, der ihn bis an seinen Tod begleitet, und sein Plato ward, mit dem feurigen Pinsel der Apokalypse ihn schildern sollen; so hätte er ihm so viel individuale Bestim-mung gegeben, dass jeder rufen müsste: "Das ist er! Johannes hat ihn gesehen."

> (Had our John, who accompanied Him until His death, and became his Plato, wished to depict Him with the fiery brush of the Apocalypse, he would have given him so much indi-vidual characterization that every one would have been obliged to exclaim: "That is he! John saw him!")

The Apostle John, then, who saw Jesus with his own eyes, and the Evangelist John who philosophized His teaching, merge in the apocalyptic style. Epic objectivity is transformed into the epic subjectivity of vision: intensity of perception and profundity of doctrine are one and the same. The extraordinary but typically romantic conjunction begins to emerge: primal historical fact can be known only through visionary eyes. The apocalyptic bard gives us the historical milieu and the milieu of Christian belief as the landscape of mythology.

The conception of the prophet-poet underwent a further crucial change before it could emerge in its fully romantic guise. As it became clear that the Evangelists were far removed in time and space from Jesus, not only the traditional idea of inspiration as coming directly from God, but the newer idea of historical authenticity was undermined. Doubts about the apostolic authorship of Revelation had always been voiced; but now, paradoxically, the very value that Lessing and Herder placed on John helped to undermine the Fourth Gospel; for towards the end of the eigh-teenth century their insistence on the Hellenistic-philosophic tone of the Gospel gave grounds for suspecting that it could not have been written in apostolic times nor even in a Judaic milieu. Further burden was thereby placed on the "visionary" element in the historical experience; yet what was the source and authority of the visionary element? Moreover, the Orientalism of the Scriptures was overwhelmingly confirmed by this new development; the increasing remoteness from the immediate environment of Jesus extended the range of Oriental references in the New Testament far beyond what had been meant by speaking of the "Orientalism" of

Hebrew poetry. The Word of God and His prophets became more and more tenuous, nonliteral, and ahistorical. Eichhorn and after him Coleridge undertook to restore "John" and canonicity in terms that were a monument to the end of dogmatic authority. The bard of the Gospels was created once again new, his historical inauthenticity the essence of his character.

Doubts about the authorship of the Book of Revelation had begun with Origen, who pointed out what bad Greek the Apocalyptic wrote, in blatant contrast to the learned and elegant Evangelist. Dionysius had cuttingly suggested that he was the John Mark who was servant of Barnabas and Paul (Acts 12:25); this would account too for his familiarity with Jewish legendary and heterodox material. Luther had rejected it; as had Semler. Michaelis, reviewing the entire tradition in his *Introduction*, concluded that the Book of Revelation should not be accounted canonical. Nearer home still, Coleridge found the view that the author of the Apocalypse could not have been John the apostle and evangelist: [Nathaniel] Lardner, for whose learning he had the highest respect, had written, "I must acknowledge that the Revelation, when compared with the apostle's unquestioned writings, has an unlikeness not easy to be accounted for."

A more popular suggestion, and one which is still accepted by the reputable commentator Austin Farrer, was that the author of Revelation was "Presbyter John." In Farrer's view, the Apostle John wrote nothing; Presbyter John wrote the Book of Revelation; and the Evangelist wrote the Epistles but was neither John.

The attribution to "Prester John" gives the greatest possible range to the undeniable Oriental provenance and connotations of the Book of Revelation. "Prester John" was thought to rule over an immense and vague area of "the East," until the Portuguese explorations had begun to show otherwise. He was held to be the Christian king of India; the Portuguese when they first landed assumed that the Hindu temples were a local form of Christianity. Indeed, most non-Muslim Asiatics were thought to be some kind of fallen Christians, so literal was the "monotheist" hypothesis. In the same way, because Alexander had penetrated to India, many local phenomena were interpreted as results of the Greek conquest; even Asoka's column was thought to have bastard Greek writing on it. As so often, the imposition of a Christian interpretation on Oriental cultures was paralleled by the imposition of a Hellenic interpretation.

Yet the vast extent of Prester John's possessions linked Christianity with numerous genuine if still half-legendary Asiatic phenomena. There was even a medieval tradition that St John himself was "the wandering Jew," the result possibly of the extension of his Oriental travels through the "Prester John" stories. "Prester John" was identified in J. Ludolphus, *A New History of Ethiopia* (1682) as an Asian king—"Prester-Chan"— who had been driven out of his kingdom by the king of the Tartars and was later wrongly regarded as an African king. Apparently the refugee king took up his abode in Abyssinia, for in Herbert's *Travels,* his chief fort was described as being at Amara, and he was given a Jewish connection: as a descendant of "Maqueda the Sabaean Queen," whose people became Jewish proselytes through the affectionate offices of Solomon. The specific place of conflict between the Tartars and the Christian king and bishop was not in China, where Kubla Khan ruled, but in India, where under the Mughal descendants of Kubla one of the great Moslem civilizations of the world developed, adorned by the wonderful "pleasure domes" described by [Sir William] Jones and the English returning from their struggles with Tipu Sultan, the last of the dynasty.

The author of the Book of Revelation, then, Christian, Moslem, and Jewish, Indian, Abyssinian, and African ruler, sage and magician, victorious and defeated, is the compendium of Oriental Christianity. Even if "Presbyter John" is stripped of his legendary empire, and is simply a historical bishop of Ephesus, he stands guard over the earliest Eastern outpost of Christianity, and is the appropriate author for the "Asiatic book" of the Bible.

Indeed, even if the author is taken to be John the Evangelist, it has been shown in overwhelmingly convincing and erudite detail from Herder to C. H. Dodd, how thoroughly permeated is the Fourth Gospel with Hellenistic thought of all kinds: with the pagan hermetic philosophies, with the work of Philo, in which the fusion of Greek with Judaic thought had already in the first century been effected, with Greek and Coptic Gnosticism. On whatever view, the Gospel of John presents a striking synthesis of Oriental thought, whether of the period just before, just after, or considerably after, the Fall of Jerusalem. As Beckwith says in his commentary, "Whoever the author of the Book of Revelation, the Book's origin is always "Asian."

Eichhorn still held that the author is John the Evangelist and Apostle. His grounds for maintaining the orthodox position, however, are of the greatest significance for the development of the mythological view of Christianity. If John the Apostle is today generally deprived of the authorship of the Book of Revelation, the way this is stated by the authoritative *Lexikon für Theologie und Kirche* ("from a dogmatic point of view" the question is declared "open") sums up the new and subtle way of handling these unsavoury facts suggested by Eichhorn and extended by Coleridge.

Eichhorn proposed a new solution to the problems raised by Michaelis over the authenticity of the Book of Revelation. Michaelis had made it a major issue, and one that threatened to block the progress of historical criticism, by holding that canonicity (and therefore inspiration) should in all cases depend on the authentic apostolic origin of the text. If this test had been applied, the resulting canon could have been hardly larger than Marcion's heretical Gnostic canon of the second century comprising Mark and three Pauline letters. If historical criticism was to hold the Gospels nonapostolic, then it had to find another test of canonicity, or put historical criticism altogether beyond the pale of theological respectability.

Eichhorn's procedure displays his usual mixture of boldness and conservative intention. He declined to enter into the controversy that had raged since the third century, saying evasively that "the *canonical authority* of the poem does not depend on the name of the author, but rather on the testimony of the early church and on its argument," "Carminis enim 'auctoritas canonica' non pendet ab auctoris nomine, sed a testimoniis potius veteris ecclesiae et ab eius argumento."

In short, Eichhorn, like [Friedrich] Schleiermacher, reversed Michaelis's rule. Canonicity was not to depend on apostolic authorship, but authorship on canonicity, in two senses, first, the tradition within the church, and second, the conformity of the doctrine with apostolic teaching. As Schleiermacher put it, a person in agreement with an Apostle's teaching "es eine ganz erlaubte Fiction ansehen konnte, dass er seine Schrift unter des Apostels Names herausgab," "could regard it as a completely permissible fiction to publish his writings under the apostle's name." The reliance on the argument of the poem went back to Semler's rather crude, though authentically Lutheran literary test of the authenticity of the contents, on the basis of which he denied the authorship of Revelation to John: it gave him no "Nährung für sein Herz," "nourishment for his heart." The doctrine of the weight of tradition is related both to Herder's stress on communal feeling rather than fact, and to the Reformation's theological bias. But tradition is understood in a totally new way: it is neither the unquestioned authority of the Church nor the unquestioned authority of the biblical text on which tradition rests, but the perpetually shifting sense within the Christian community of what has the power to persuade its members and strengthen them in the faith. Coleridge was to develop these two, still embryonic, approaches into one in his later writings: whatever the literal, documentable truth might be found to be, the historical experience of conviction within the Christian community was in itself a form of validation, and this experience could be maintained and reawakened through an imaginative grasp of what that experience had been. Apostolic authorship depended on canonicity, and canonicity ultimately on inspiration in the new sense of the capacity to recreate imaginatively the experience of faith.

These concerns were, of course, at the centre of romantic aesthetics. The need for imaginative reconstruction of events which could not be reliably known in any other way led directly to the elaboration of the poet's power to recreate and the audience's ability to share in the poetic process. The issue was raised in the classical essay on biblical hermeneutics, J. A. Ernesti's *Institutio Interpretis Novi Testamenti* (1761), translated in 1832 as *Principles of Biblical Interpretation*. Hermeneutics is the general principles of interpretation of texts; interpretation is exegesis, or application of principles. Ernesti wrote simply:

> Interpretation is the art of teaching the real sentiment contained in any form of words, or of effecting that another may derive from them the same idea that the writer intended to convey.

Schleiermacher, meditating on Ernesti early in the nineteenth century, posed the question at a more philosophical level: What is it to understand? Under what conditions is *Verstehen* possible? Until Schleiermacher, hermeneutics was only "ein Gebäude der Regeln," "an edifice of rules," as [Wilhelm] Dilthey put it. Even Ernesti, although he started from purely linguistic considerations, suggested the scope of the enterprise: the interpreter must not only know the biblical languages, he must possess "distinguished attainments, in antiquities, history, chronology, in short, in all liberal knowledge and critical art." Schleiermacher called for an "allgemeine Hermeneutik," a "general hermeneutics." This required not simply the application of textual rules, but the "Nachbildung eines fremden Lebens," "the reconstruction of alien experience," the experience of the author within his historical milieu. Schleiermacher drew on Winckelmann's art criticism, on Herder's mode of empathy with earlier periods, and on the new aesthetic philosophy of Heyne and F. A. Wolf, as well as on Friedrich Schlegel, who had planned an *ars critica* grounded in a theory of the productive literary capacity, illustrated by his essays on Greek poetry, on Goethe, on Boccaccio. The philosophical underpinnings of his general hermeneutics he borrowed from Schelling, especially the *Vor-*

lesungen über die Methode des akademischen Studiums (1802), *Lectures on the Methods of University Studies*. Briefly stated, "art is *the* instrument whereby empirical history is possible." To put it another way, only art can hold out the hope that "Past thoughts can be re-enacted in the minds of the historians."

Dilthey described the major accomplishment of Schleiermacher's hermeneutics in these terms:

> Sie soll gegenüber dem beständigen Einbruch romantischer Willkür und skeptischer Subjektivität in das Gebiet der Geschichte die Allgemeingültigkeit der Interpretation theoretisch begründen, auf welcher aller Sicherheit der Geschichte beruht.

> (The function of hermeneutics, as against the continuous intrusion of romantic arbitrariness and sceptical subjectivity into the domain of history, is to provide a theoretical grounding for the general validity of the interpretation, on which all historical certainty rests.)

> ("Die Enstellung der Hermeneutik")

But Dilthey spoke as the founder of the *Geisteswissenschaften,* of the modern social sciences, as one concerned with finding an "objectivity" to rank with (though not identical with) that claimed by the natural sciences. Dilthey, then, distorted Schleiermacher in borrowing romantic techniques of empathy and of recreation in order to ground a new claim to objectivity for the historical sciences. For the romantics there was no guarantee of objectivity; sceptical subjectivity was at the basis of the need to have recourse to the poetic reconstruction of past experience.

The recourse to art for explanation, for *Verstehen,* became a programme for art. In "The Ancient Mariner," Coleridge drew a visionary character belonging clearly to the primitive milieu in which apostolic credulity could flourish. These were the apostles as the *Wolfenbüttel Fragmente* described them—poor, deprived, ill-educated men, subject to accesses of superstitious fear and reverance. And these were the apostles as Herder described them, primitive bards telling a tale destined to be repeated over and over again, and winning an audience in the most unlikely places. The poem wholly conveys the authenticity of the incredible event in the psyche of the teller, which is unassailable, and has the power of communicating itself to others.

Coleridge could not have known Schleiermacher's lectures on hermeneutics directly, for they were not published until 1838; but he had the same background in biblical criticism, and there is no doubt he attempted to find a historical art of interpretation that would lend the poise of objectivity to the subjective process of "Nachbildung eines fremden Lebens." In the *Aids to Reflection,* Coleridge attempted to reconstruct the mode of thought of Archbishop Leighton, and with it the milieu of seventeenth-century Christian belief, in order both to point up what was out of reach of contemporary Christianity, and exactly in that measure to restore it. Taking contemporary reason as his guide, he could convey the inwardness of doctrine only through reconstruction of a remote experience.

The peculiar connection of dubiety and creativity is summed up in the character of the apocalyptic. The apocalyptic is by definition a false prophet. In Jewish thought "there was no true apocalyptic until prophecy failed" (Frank Kermode, *The Sense of an Ending*). The writer of apocalyptic uses the methods and style and tone of the true prophets, and often he borrows the very name of a genuine prophet. The "prophecy" is written after the fact: it uses a known occurrence of destruction, an undeniable doom, on which to base its predictions of still greater catastrophe, or the end of the world. Its accuracy about the "predicted" but past event buys the prophet credit.

Those who wished to maintain the authenticity of Revelation have always narrowed the distinction between true prophecy and apocalypse as much as possible, even in some cases claiming superiority for apocalypse as a form developed relatively late in Jewish history. Eichhorn, and even more Coleridge, gave another twist to this. By extension, all the biblical rhapsodes become "apocalyptics" if none is apostolic. In short, all are poets assuming an apostolic name. The Book of Revelation is placed on a par with the Gospels, is canonical once more in this entirely new sense of the word. Canonicity depends on the capacity of the text to undergo and to call forth continued imaginative reconstruction of the *Urevangelium* within it.

It is here that the poet Coleridge soars out beyond the rationalist Eichhorn. In opposition to the deist contention that ancient religious leaders were tricksters, Eichhorn offered a still rationalist though historicized defence: they worked in the spirit of their age; they were not fraudulent, but unavoidably credulous. Eichhorn treated the great prophets as conscious artists, bridging the gap between the Enlightenment charges of deliberate fraud and straightforward orthodox claims to divine inspiration. This was a brilliant solution. Yet there is more than a trace of the notion of deliberate trickery left in Eichhorn's conception of the artist.

Ezekiel he praises as the greatest artist of the prophets—and therefore the least authentic visionary: "Alle Entzückungen und Visionen sind, meinem Urtheil nach, blosse Einkleidung, blosse poetische Dichtungen." "All these raptures and visions are in my judgement mere cover-up, mere poetical fancies." Coleridge protested against this unwarranted distinction between the artist and the visionary:

> It perplexes me to understand how a Man of Eichhorn's Sense, Learning, and Acquaintance with Psychology could form, or attach belief to, so cold-blooded an hypothesis. That in Ezeckiel's Visions Ideas or Spiritual Entities are presented in visual Symbols, I never doubted; but as little can I doubt, that such Symbols did present themselves to Ezekiel in Visions—and by a Law closely connected with, if not contained in, that by which Sensations are organized into Images and Mental Sounds in our ordinary sleep.
>
> (Marginal note to Eichhorn)

Ezekiel's vision of God, Eichhorn claimed, is "so magnificent, varied, and great that the presentation can hardly be an impromptu, but must have been planned and worked out with much art." "So mahlt, z. B. Ezechiel seine Gotteserscheinung so prächtig, vielseitig und gross, dass schwerlich ihre Darstellung ein Impromptu sein kann, sondern von ihm mit Kunst angelegt und ausgearbeitet sein muss." In a splendid marginal note, Coleridge demurs, offering his own experience as evidence:

> From the analogy of Dreams during an excited state of the Nerves, which I have myself experienced, and the wonderful intricacy, complexity, and yet clarity of the visual Objects, I should infer the contrary. Likewise, the noticeable fact of the words descriptive of these Objects rising at the same time, and with the same spontaneity and absence of all conscious Effort, weighs greatly with me, against the hypothesis of Pre-meditation, in this and similar Passages of the Prophetic Books.

He made the same objection to Eichhorn's dismissal of certain passages of Revelation as mere poetic embroidery. Where the tradition and the training of the seer is sufficiently strong, where he is saturated in the spiritual experience of his community, his visions can be spontaneous, not artfully premeditated. So too the poet's imagination, steeped in its own subject, may compose as if inspired.

The claim Coleridge made in his preface to "Kubla" to a form of spontaneous composition is not an excuse for a fragment, but a presentation of his credentials for writing apocalyptic, for assuming the prophetic role. In however small a degree, he could claim to have shared the experience of the great prophets, of Ezekiel, and of the great apocalyptic, John. These experiences were in one form or another so persistent with Coleridge, and figure so largely in his theory of the imagination, that his account of the writing of "Kubla" should not be dismissed as a figment. Each rift of his mind loaded with the ore of the Apocalypse, Southey's Oriental enthusiasms, his own epic plans and hopes, the first tentative notions of the lyrical ballads, and experiments in versification, it is perfectly possible that he should have dreamed the whole in this vivid compressed form in which all the major images are concentrated and blent, and the action concentrated at the point most pregnant with its own significance: the creation of the holy city threatened with destruction and promised its recreation. The prefatory "Vision in a Dream" becomes a kind of authentication of the poet's right to present the prophetic lays of a "John."

Now that inspiration was not directly divine, now that it must take place without miracle, "without any sensible addition or infusion," the sources of vision must be such as would satisfy the Enlightenment rationalists as well as fulfil some part of the traditional expectations. Coleridge's preface is apologetical, in that it claims none but natural phenomena behind a psychological curiosity, while the state described approximates as nearly as possible to illuminated trance and supernatural dictation.

Among the forms of suspension of the conditions of ordinary perception which played so important a role in Coleridge's theory of the imagination, sleep (or waking dreams) is prominent:

> In the paradisiacal World Sleep was voluntary & holy—a spiritual before God, in which the mind elevated by contemplation retired into pure intellect suspending all commerce with sensible objects & perceiving the present deity.
>
> (*Notebooks*)

Sleep (and anodynes for physical pain) are most readily grasped by the Enlightened mind as altering mental conditions, yet all such suspension, with the insertion of the vivid but ultimately vague (alliterating) detail— the haunting "person from Porlock"—strengthens the visionary claim, and is part of the apocalyptic method.

In the new secular theory of inspiration, then—and this was its triumph—there was no difference between the brief note on the Crewe [manuscript] of "Kubla" and the later, more elaborate prefatory "Vision in a Dream." Still later, in his *Confessions*, Coleridge wrote of the welcome confirmation that the Bible tradition gave to the visitations of the "phantom self":

> The Bible has been found a spiritual World,—spiritual, and yet at the same time outward and common to all. You in one place, I in another, all men somewhere or at some time, meet with an assurance that the hopes and fears, the thoughts and yearnings that proceed from or tend to, a right spirit in us, are not dreams or fleeting singularities, no voices heard in sleep, or spectres which the eye suffers but not perceives.

Coleridge never wished to exploit this element of falsehood and pose (the irony appealed to some poets of his time and after), except in so far as it rendered prophecy, like all the bardic gifts, remote and unattainable in its true form. Strain and yearning characterized the poetic assumption of the prophetic attitude. Just as Coleridge refused to hold that the great religious sages and leaders had deliberately deceived the people, so the illicit and deliberate assumption of powers by the traditional apocalyptic was represented only in the great contortions and involutions of the poet seeking a vision closed to him.

The romantic longing to approximate the seer reached its apotheosis in Rimbaud's famous letter:

> I say that one must be a *seer,* make oneself a *seer.* The poet makes himself a *seer* by a long, prodigious and rational *disordering of all the senses.* Every form of love, of suffering, of madness; he searches himself, he consumes all the poisons in him, and keeps only their quintessences. This is an unspeakable torture during which he needs all his faith and superhuman strength, and during which he becomes the great patient, the great criminal, the great accursed—and the great banned one!—among men. For he arrives at the *unknown!*
>
> (Letter to Paul Demeny, 1871)

Rimbaud spoke somewhat contemptuously of the earlier generation:

> The first romantics were seers without quite realizing it: the cultivation of their souls began accidentally: abandoned locomotives, but with their fires still alight, which the rails still carry along for a while.

But this was hardly the case: Coleridge's generation first grasped rationally the necessity to "cultivate their souls," and stoked those fires as assiduously as Rimbaud, while pretending, at times, to be carried along on the rails. The apocalyptic seer, while claiming more than the poet, is closer to the poet than the true prophet; he perfectly represents the romantic union of despair of true vision with the inflation of the poetic imagination. Prophecy having failed—the true visionary having vanished—the poetic genre of apocalypse must take its place, and the false prophet, the poet, do his best to speak truth, though only in symbols figuring the throne and face of God he cannot see, and dimly reminiscent of the origins of prophetic and poetic knowledge in the first radiance of mythological prehistory.

And yet, were not the first apocalyptics and rhapsodes of the Gospel in the same position as the poet? The direct apostolic vision was only a shred of memory long after a "fact" that had never been. The romantics achieved a new comprehension not only of their own historical position, but of the problematic nature of all the seers of the past. In the terms of their own analysis, they were able genuinely to revive the conditions of inspiration.

Thus Coleridge's prophet-poet, if still Greek, still "Pindaric" in feeling and reference, is equally the Renaissance David, the classic David of Michelangelo, and the Christian John, humane and sophisticated; and in his anonymity, behind these great Oriental figures, is visible the universal primitive bard, the bard of the Tartars and of the Celts and of the Americans, the bard of the Neoplatonic mysteries and of the early Christians, a bizarre, rapt creature maintaining for his community their touch with the nether and the upper worlds. And the modern poet justly stands here too: for romanticism calls all vision in question, while affirming it.

If, then, we accord to Coleridge the poetic vision of the apocalyptic as he redefined it, the form in which he accomplished his epic of revelation is not difficult to understand. If religious epic in the eighteenth century had taken on the characteristics of the ode, on the model of *Samson* or the *Messias,* the brief, almost static action, interspersed with choric song, the theory, authoritatively formulated by Wolf in his *Prolegomena ad Homerum* (1795), that the *Iliad* was not Homer's, but a redaction of a series of lays handed down in folk tradition, offered an obvious new form for the deliberate production of epic, especially to a masterly practitioner of the ballad, the "obvious British equivalent of the hypothetical Homeric rhapsodes." As Albert Friedman has pointed out in *The Ballad Revival,*

In the neo-classic period, the ancient writings about bards and

> rhapsodes, about commemorative and chronicle verse, were used to comment on the ballads; but after the ballad had actually been found in tradition, the flow of instruction was reversed, and the balladry emerged as a striking clue to the perplexing problem of Homer and the homeridae.

In the same way, balladry emerged as a striking clue to the problem of the composition of the Bible.

For apocalypse, where one could expect no straightforward consecutive narrative, the ballad-lay was the ideal solution, excising all epic flats and bringing the bard figure to the fore. Scott in the "Lay of the Last Minstrel," so notoriously inspired by "Christabel," and Macaulay's "Lays of Ancient Rome" tried to do just this: to take a historical and heroic matter, fit stuff for an epic, and render it in the "original" folk form of the lay. Macaulay based his "Lays of Ancient Rome" (1842) both on Wolf's Homeric ballad theory and on Niebuhr's argument in his *Roman History* (1811–15, translated in part by Coleridge's "disciples" Thirlwall and Hare in 1828–30) that traditional lays were the source of the legendary portions of Roman history in Livy's *Annales,* "broken and defaced fragments of the early poetry," as Macaulay put it. Thomas Arnold, who helped make Niebuhr's a powerful influence, espoused this idea, and Macaulay undertook to recast Livy's legendary material in what must have been, according to Niebuhr, its original form.

As Friedman has remarked, "Both Wolf and Niebuhr were aware that their theories reflected on the composition of Holy Scriptures." Their theories ultimately rest on Herder's argument in *The Spirit of Hebrew Poetry* that the creation story had evolved from primitive folksongs, from isolated ballads "On the Sabbath," "On the Destruction of the World," and so on. Coleridge's substantial agreement is shown by his proposal for "a metrical translation of all the odes and fragments of odes scattered throughout the Pentateuch and the Historical works of the O. Testament." This conception of Homer as bard connected him intimately with the Prophets.

Macaulay's notion of the ancient lay is represented by this strophe:

> And nearer fast and nearer
>   Doth the red whirlwind come;
> And louder still and still more loud
> From underneath that rolling cloud,
> Is heard the trumpet's war-note proud
>   The trampling and the hum.

And plainly and more plainly
  Now through the gloom appears,
Far to left and far to right,
In broken gleams of dark-blue light,
The long array of helmets bright,
  The long array of spears.
              ("Horatius," 21)

In the English tradition, the ode had tended to be closer to the ballad than elsewhere. Drayton in a minor lyric gives the history of the ode, including the Greek, the Druid, and the ancient British Harper. His own "Agincourt" is a sophisticated ballad, a welding together of native and foreign elements. Moreover, he wrote that though he called his poems "odes," they might be called "ballads"; this seems to have been the result of a confusion of "ballad" with "ballade": "For both the great Master of Italian rymes [*sic*], PETRARCH, and our CHAUCER and others of the Upper House of the Muses, have thought their Canzons honoured in the title of a Ballad." Thomas Warton's influential *History of English Poetry* referred to some Anglo-Saxon and Middle English poems as "odes," especially the "Battle of Brunanburgh" and the "Poema Morale."

Donald Davie was evidently mistaken in asserting that there is "no precedent in English" for the marriage of the ode and the ballad that Ezra Pound effected in *The Confucian Odes*. Rather Pound discovered in the ancient Chinese confirmation of the romantic enterprise of the lyrical ballad.

Given the Apocalypse as epic matter, the new theory perfectly accounts for the form of "Kubla": a fusion between a traditional ballad form, with its sense of essential rhythms and consonances, and the irregular, "sublime" ode forms, which raised the minstrel into a rhapsode.

The combination of ballad-lay and ode conforms to the twofold nature of the new romantic bard. The ballad preserves the contact with the original primitive folk community out of which epic, whether the *Iliad* or the *New Testament,* sprung, embodying its mythologized historical experience; the ode expresses that society's highest pitch and reach of religious development. In Wordsworth's hands, the lyrical ballad never attained the same fusion; it tended to separate out into the familiar eighteenth-century forms of the pseudopopular ballad and the meditative ode.

Coleridge's dream-vision tale is substantially true, then, and he wrote not one lay of his intended epic, but a kind of symbolic summary of its entire action and significance. It was indeed a fragment of a vast intention; and yet a whole poem. Just as Coleridge developed a method of asserting the unity of Bible texts despite their disintegration in time and space, so he created a new epic unity despite the fragmentary "lay theory" of Homer. "Kubla Khan," the apocalyptic epic, is the apotheosis of a new form: the lyrical ballad.

Chronology

	TEXTUAL		HISTORICAL

		?	The Creation and the Flood
		1800 B.C.E.	The Patriarchs and the Sojourn in Egypt (ca. 1800–1250)
		1700 B.C.E.	
		1600 B.C.E.	
		1500 B.C.E.	
		1400 B.C.E.	
		1300 B.C.E.	
		1200 B.C.E.	The Exodus and the Conquest (ca. 1250–1200) Joshua (ca. 1200–1150) The Judges (ca. 1150–1025)
		1100 B.C.E.	The Monarchy (ca. 1025–930)
The J Source (ca. 950–900)		1000 B.C.E.	The Two Kingdoms (ca. 930–590)

TEXTUAL

HISTORICAL

900 B.C.E.

The E Source (ca. 850–800)

800 B.C.E.

Amos, Proverbs 10–22:16 (ca. 750)
Hosea (ca. 725)
Micah, Proverbs 25–29, Isaiah 1–31, JE redaction (ca. 700)

The Fall of Samaria (ca. 720)
The Reformation of Josiah (ca. 700–600)

700 B.C.E.

Deuteronomy, Zephaniah (ca. 650)
Nahum, Proverbs 22:17–24 (ca. 625)
Deuteronomy-Kings (ca. 600–500), Jeremiah, Habakkuk (ca. 600)

The Fall of Jerusalem and the Exile to Babylonia (ca. 587–538)

600 B.C.E.

Job 3–31, 38–42:6 (ca. 575)
Isaiah 40–55, Job 32–37 (ca. 550)
Isaiah 56–66, Jeremiah 46–52, Ezekiel 1–37, 40–48, Lamentations (ca. 525)

The Return (ca. 538)

Job redaction, the P Source, Haggai, Zechariah 1–8, Jeremiah 30–31 (ca. 500)

500 B.C.E.

Additions to Ezekiel 1–37, 40–48 (ca. 475–400)
Joel, Malachi, Proverbs 30–31, Lists (ca. 450)
JEP redaction [Genesis-Numbers], Isaiah 32–35, Proverbs 1–9, Ruth, Obadiah (ca. 425)

Nehemiah and Ezra (ca. 475–350)

JEPD redaction, Jonah, Psalms, Proverbs redaction, Song of Songs, Chronicles, Ezra, Nehemiah (ca. 400)

400 B.C.E.

Ecclesiastes (ca. 350)

The Hellenistic Period (ca. 330–63)

TEXTUAL		HISTORICAL
Zechariah 9–14 (ca. 325)	300 B.C.E.	
Isaiah 24–27, Ezekiel 38–39 (ca. 300)		
The Septuagint, a translation of the Hebrew Bible into Greek (ca. 250–100)		
	200 B.C.E.	
Daniel (ca. 175)		The Maccabean Revolt (ca. 165)
Esther (ca. 100)	100 B.C.E.	
		Pompey takes Jerusalem (ca. 63)
	10 B.C.E.	
		Birth of Christ (ca. 6)
	B.C.E.	
	C.E.	
	10 C.E.	
	20 C.E.	
		Baptism of Christ and the beginning of John's Ministry (ca. 26)
	30 C.E.	Crucifixion of Christ and Pentecost (ca. 30)
		Conversion of Paul (ca. 32)
	40 C.E.	Martyrdom of James (ca. 44)
		Paul and Barnabas visit Jerusalem during famine (ca. 46)
Galatians (ca. 49)		Paul's First Missionary Journey (ca. 47–48)
Thessalonian Letters (ca. 50)	50 C.E.	Paul's Second Missionary Journey (ca. 49–52)
Corinthian Letters (ca. 53–55)		Paul's Third Missionary Journey (ca. 52–56)

131

TEXTUAL		HISTORICAL
		Paul arrested in Jerusalem and imprisoned by Caesar (ca. 56–58)
Romans (ca. 56)		
		Paul's voyage to Rome and shipwreck (ca. 58)
	60 C.E.	First Roman imprisonment of Paul (ca. 59–60)
Philippians (ca. 60)		Paul's release and last travels (ca. 61–63)
Colossians, Philemon (ca. 61–62)		Paul's second Roman imprisonment and martyrdom (ca. 64–65)
Mark (ca. 65–67)		Death of Peter (ca. 64–65)
	70 C.E.	Fall of Jerusalem (ca. 70)
	80 C.E.	
Matthew (ca. 75–80)	90 C.E.	
Canonization of the Hebrew Bible at Synod of Jamnia (ca. 90)		Persecutions under Emperor Domitian discussed in Revelation (ca. 93–96)
Ephesians, Hebrews, Revelation, Luke, Acts (ca. 95); 1 Peter (ca. 95–100), Fourth Gospel (ca. 95–115)	100 C.E.	
Johannine Epistles (ca. 110–115)	125 C.E.	
James, Jude (ca. 125–150)	150 C.E.	
2 Peter (ca. 150)		
Timothy, Titus (ca. 160–175)	175 C.E.	
	200 C.E.	

TEXTUAL

300 C.E.

400 C.E.

500 C.E.
600 C.E.
700 C.E.
800 C.E.
900 C.E.
1000 C.E.
1100 C.E.
1200 C.E.
1300 C.E.

1400 C.E.

1500 C.E.

Stabilization of the New Testament canon of twenty-seven books (ca. 350–400)

Jerome completes the Latin Vulgate, a translation of the Bible based on the Septuagint and translated from the Hebrew (ca. 400)

The first translation of the Bible into English, by John Wycliffe (ca. 1382)

The Gutenberg Bible printed from movable type, ushering in the new era of printing (1456)

Erasmus finishes a translation of the Bible into Greek (1516)

Martin Luther translates the Bible into German (1522)

William Tyndale's and Miles Coverdale's English translations of the Bible (1535)

TEXTUAL

Matthew's Bible produced, based on the Tyndale
and Coverdale versions (1537)
The Great Bible produced by Coverdale (1539)
The Geneva Bible, the first to separate chapters
into verses (1560)
The Douay-Rheims Bible, a Catholic translation
from Latin into English (1582–1610)
The King James Version completed (1611)

1600 C.E.

1700 C.E.

1800 C.E.

The English Revised Version coissued by English
and American scholars (1885)
The American Standard Version (1901)
The Moffatt Bible (1924)
The Smith–Goodspeed Bible (1931)
The Confraternity Version, an Episcopal revision
of the Douay-Rheims Bible (1941)
Knox's Version, based on the Latin Vulgate and
authorized by the Catholic Church (1945–49)
The Revised Standard Version (1952)
The New English Bible, Protestant (1961)
The Jerusalem Bible, Catholic (1966)
The Modern Language Bible (1969)
The New American Bible, Catholic (1970)
Today's English Version (1976)
The New International Version (1978)
The New Jewish Version (1982)

1900 C.E.

Contributors

HAROLD BLOOM, Sterling Professor of the Humanities at Yale University, is the author of *The Anxiety of Influence, Poetry and Repression,* and many other volumes of literary criticism. His forthcoming study, *Freud: Transference and Authority,* attempts a full-scale reading of all of Freud's major writings. A MacArthur Prize Fellow, he is general editor of five series of literary criticism published by Chelsea House. During 1987–88, he served as Charles Eliot Norton Professor of Poetry at Harvard University.

M. H. ABRAMS is Class of 1916 Professor of English at Cornell University. His many works of literary criticism include *The Mirror and the Lamp: Romantic Theory and the Critical Tradition, A Glossary of Literary Terms,* and *Natural Supernaturalism: Tradition and Revolution in Romantic Literature.*

JOHN R. MAY is Professor of English at Louisiana State University. He is the author of several works including *Toward a New Earth: Apocalypse and the American Novel* and *The Pruning Word: The Parables of Flannery O'Connor.*

D. H. LAWRENCE, novelist, poet, and critic, is best known for his novels *Sons and Lovers, The Rainbow,* and *Women in Love.* His *Studies in Classic American Literature* may be the single most illuminating book on American literary imagination.

AUSTIN FARRER was Doctor of Divinity and Fellow of Trinity College at Oxford. His books include *A Rebirth of Images: The Making of St. John's Apocalypse, Finite and Infinite: A Philosophical Essay,* and *The Freedom of the Will.*

NORTHROP FRYE, University Professor Emeritus at the University of Toronto, is one of this century's most influential literary critics. His principal works are *Fearful Symmetry, Anatomy of Criticism,* and *The Great Code.*

ADELA YARBRO COLLINS teaches in the Department of New Testament at McCormick Theological Seminary. She is the author of *Apocalypse* in the New Testament Message Series and *Crisis and Catharsis: The Power of Apocalypse.*

E. S. SHAFFER is Reader in Modern Languages and European History at the University of East Anglia. She is the author of *"Kubla Khan" and The Fall of Jerusalem: The Mythological School in Biblical Criticism and Secular Literature, 1770–1880.*

Bibliography

Barr, David L. "The Apocalypse as a Symbolic Transformation of the World: A Literary Analysis" *Interpretation* 38 (January 1984): 39–50.

Beardslee, William A. "Hope in Biblical Eschatology and in Process Theology." *Journal of the American Academy of Religion* 38 (1970): 227–39.

———. *Literary Criticism in the New Testament.* Philadelphia: Fortress Press, 1970.

Beckwith, Isbon T. *The Apocalypse of John: Studies in Introduction with a Critical and Exegetical Commentary.* New York: Macmillan, 1919.

Bowman, John W. "The Revelation to John: Its Dramatic Structure and Message." *Interpretation* 9 (1955): 436–53.

———. *The First Christian Drama: The Book of Revelation.* Philadelphia: Westminster Press, 1968.

Buber, Martin. *Pointing the Way.* New York: Harper & Row, 1963.

Caird, G. B. *A Commentary on the Revelation of St. John the Divine.* New York: Harper & Row, 1966.

Carter, Frederick. "Drama and Apocalypse." *Life and Letters* 60 (1949): 221–29.

Charles, R. H. *A Critical and Exegetical Commentary on the Revelation of St. John.* New York: Scribner's, 1920.

———. *Eschatology: The Doctrine of a Future Life in Israel, Judaism, and Christianity.* New York: Schocken, 1963.

Collins, Adela Yarbro. *Crisis and Catharsis: The Power of the Apocalypse.* Philadelphia: Westminster Press, 1984.

Collins, John J. *The Apocalyptic Vision of the Book of Daniel.* Missoula, Mont.: Scholars Press, 1977.

Derrida, Jacques. "Of an Apocalyptic Tone Recently Adopted in Philosophy." Translated by John P. Leavy, Jr. In *Derrida and Biblical Studies,* edited by Robert Detweiler, 63–98. *Semeia* 23. Baltimore: Scholars Press, 1982.

Farrer, Austin. *A Rebirth of Images: The Making of St. John's Apocalypse.* Boston: Beacon Press, 1963.

Feuillet, Andre. *The Apocalypse.* New York: Alba House, 1965.

Fiorenza, Elisabeth Schussler. *The Book of Revelation—Justice and Judgement.* Philadelphia: Fortress Press, 1985.

Furia, Philip. "'IS, the whited monster': Lowell's Quaker Graveyard Revisited." *Texas Studies in Literature and Language* 17 (1976): 837–54.

Hanson, Paul D. *The Dawn of Apocalyptic.* Philadelphia: Fortress Press, 1975.

Helms, Randall. "Blake's Use of the Bible in 'A Song of Liberty.'" *English Language Notes* 16 (1979): 287–91.

Jones, Bruce W. "More about the Apocalypse as Apocalyptic." *Journal of Biblical Literature* 87 (1968): 325–27.

Jones, Rufus M. *The Eternal Gospel*. New York: Macmillan, 1938.

Juel, Donald, James S. Ackerman, and Thayer S. Warshaw. *An Introduction to New Testament Literature*. Nashville, Tenn.: Abingdon Press, 1978.

Kallas, James. "The Apocalypse—An Apocalyptic Book?" *Journal of Biblical Literature* 86 (1967): 69–80.

Kepler, Thomas S. *The Book of Revelation: A Commentary for Laymen*. New York: Oxford University Press, 1957.

Kermode, Frank. *The Sense of an Ending: Studies in the Theory of Fiction*. New York: Oxford University Press, 1967.

Koch, Klaus. *The Rediscovery of the Apocalypse*. Translated by Margaret Kohl. London: SCM Press, 1972.

Lerner, Robert. "Antichrists and Antichrist in Joachim of Fiore." *Speculum* 60 (July 1985): 553–70.

Lewicki, Zbigniew. *Bang and the Whimper: Apocalypse and Entropy in American Literature*. Westport, Conn.: Greenwood, 1984.

Lewis, R. W. B. "Days of Wrath and Laughter." In *Trials of the Word: Essays in American Literature and the Humanistic Tradition*. New Haven: Yale University Press, 1965.

MacQueen, John. "Biblical Allegory." In *Allegory*. London: Methuen, 1970.

Moltmann, Jürgen. *Theology of Hope*. New York: Harper & Row, 1967.

O'Day, Gail R. *Revelation in the Fourth Gospel: Narrative Mode and Theological Chain*. Philadelphia: Fortress Press, 1986.

Patrides, C. A. "'Something Like Prophetic Strain': Apocalyptic Configurations in Milton." *English Language Notes* 19 (1982): 193–207.

Patrides, C. A., and Joseph Anthony Wittreich, Jr., eds. *The Apocalypse in English Renaissance Literature*. Ithaca: Cornell University Press, 1983.

Revard, Stella P. "The Warring Saints and the Dragon: A Commentary upon Revelation 12:7–9 and Milton's War in Heaven." *Philological Quarterly* 53 (1974): 181–94.

Robinson, Douglas. *American Apocalypses: The Image of the End of the World in American Literature*. Baltimore: Johns Hopkins University Press, 1985.

Rowley, H. H. *The Relevance of Apocalyptic: A Study of Jewish and Christian Apocalypse from Daniel to the Revelation*. 1944. Rev. ed. London: Lutterworth Press, 1963.

Ryan, Robert. "Christ and Moneta." *English Language Notes* 13 (1976): 190–92.

Swete, Henry Barclay. *The Apocalypse of St. John*. London: Macmillan, 1907.

Turner, N. "Revelation." In *Peake's Commentary on the Bible,* edited by Matthew Black and H. H. Rowley. London: Thomas Nelson & Sons, 1962.

Tuveson, Ernest Lee. *Millennium and Utopia: A Study in the Background of the Idea of Progress*. New York: Harper & Row, 1964.

Unnik, W. C. van. "'Worthy is the Lamb': The Background of Apocalypse 5." In *Mélanges bibliques en hommage au R. P. Beda Rigaux,* edited by A. Deschamps and A. de Halleux. Gembloux, Belgium: Duculot, 1970.

Wakeman, Mary K. *God's Battle with the Monster: A Study in Biblical Imagery.* Leiden, Netherlands: Brill, 1973.

Wallace, Howard. "Leviathan and the Beast in Revelation." In *The Biblical Archeologist Reader.* Vol. 1, edited by G. Ernest Wright and David Noel Freedman. Garden City, N.Y.: Doubleday, 1961.

Acknowledgments

"Apocalypse: Theme and Romantic Variations" by M. H. Abrams from *The Correspondent Breeze: Essays on English Romanticism* by M. H. Abrams, © 1984 by M. H. Abrams and Jack Stillinger. Reprinted by permission of Cornell University Press and Manchester University Press. This essay first appeared in *The Apocalypse in English Renaissance Thought and Literature,* edited by C. A. Patrides and Joseph A. Wittreich, Jr.

"The Judaeo-Christian Apocalypse" (originally entitled "Apocalypse and the American Tradition") by John R. May from *Toward a New Earth: Apocalypse in the American Novel* by John R. May, © 1972 by the University of Notre Dame Press. Reprinted by permission.

"Apocalypse" by D. H. Lawrence from *Apocalypse* by D. H. Lawrence, edited by Mara Kalnins, © 1931 by the Estate of David Herbert Lawrence, © 1980 by the Estate of Frieda Lawrence Ravagli. Reprinted by permission of Viking Penguin, Inc.

"A Rebirth of Images: The Kingdom of Darkness" (originally entitled "Chapter 11") by Austin Farrer from *A Rebirth of Images: The Making of St. John's Apocalypse* by Austin Farrer, © 1963 by Dacre Press. Reprinted by permission of the State University of New York Press and the Trust of Mrs. K. D. Fasves Deceased.

"Typology: Apocalypse" (originally entitled "Typology II: Phases of Revelation") by Northrop Frye from *The Great Code: The Bible and Literature* by Northrop Frye, © 1981, 1982 by Northrop Frye. Reprinted by permission of Harcourt Brace Jovanovich, Inc.

"The Power of Apocalyptic Rhetoric-Catharsis" by Adela Yarbro Collins from *Crisis and Catharsis: The Power of Apocalypse* by Adela Yarbro Collins, © 1984 by Adela Yarbro Collins. Reprinted and used by permission of The Westminster Press.

"The Visionary Character: Revelation and the Lyrical Ballad" by E. S. Shaffer from *"Kubla Khan" and* The Fall of Jerusalem: *The Mythological School in Biblical Criticism and Secular Literature, 1770–1880* by E. S. Shaffer, © 1975 by Cambridge University Press. Reprinted by permission of Cambridge University Press.

Index

Absolutes: Blake and, 12; Hegel and, 14; Neoplatonism and, 13; in Revelation, 11–12; Schelling and, 14, 30–31

Aesthetic Education of Man (Schiller), 30

Ages of the World, The (Schelling), 32

Aggression, in Revelation, 4–5, 47, 88–90, 93–94

"Agincourt" (Drayton), 127

Ahab, and the false prophets, 58

Aids to Reflection (Coleridge), 121

Allegory: in Daniel, 46; in Revelation, 45–47, 69, 74–75, 79; Revelation as, 20. *See also* Literary symbolism

America, as the New Jerusalem, 24–25

American imperialism, apocalypticism and, 24–25

American Revolution, and apocalypticism, 18

Anabaptist movement: and apocalypticism, 18; John of Leyden and, 18; Müntzer and, 18

Antichrist, the: identification of, 19, 47, 62–63; nature of, 56–57, 62–64, 65, 66–67

Anticlassical interpretation, of Revelation, 98–99

Apocalypse: Christianity and necessity for, 49–50, 70–71; Ezra and, 37; Farrer on, 39; Rufus Jones on, 14–15; in Judaism, 35–37, 38, 39, 41; meaning of word, 1, 8, 69; Milton on, 19; nature of, 11, 14–15, 38–39, 40, 70–71; and prophecy, 36, 37, 69, 77–79; and revolution, 18; as theme in Western literature, 2; Wilder on, 40; Zealots and, 75

Apocalypticism: and American imperialism, 24–25; American Revolution and, 18; Anabaptists and, 18; Beardslee on, 38; Cromwell and, 18; in Daniel, 9; in Exodus, 9, 79; French Revolution and, 18, 26–28; in Genesis, 9; and the Gospels, 20; interpretation of, 19–20; and Marxist theory of absolute revolution, 18–19; Milton and, 18; nature of, 88; Rimbaud on, 124; romanticism and, 25–27, 28–31, 32–33, 125; and schizophrenia, 87–88; and scholasticism, 40, 56; as theme in the Bible, 14; as theme in Western civilization, 8–10, 11, 13–14, 15–16, 18–20, 24–28, 32–33; as threat to the established Church, 15; William Gilpin and, 25

Aristotle, and meaning of catharsis, 85

Armageddon: battle of, 10, 12, 57–58, 65, 67; location of, 58

Athanasius, *Life of St. Anthony,* 20

"Attempt to Estimate the Poetical Talent of the Present Age, An" (Talfourd), 27

143